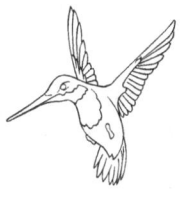

Dedicated to my family,
Debi, Caleb and Morgan

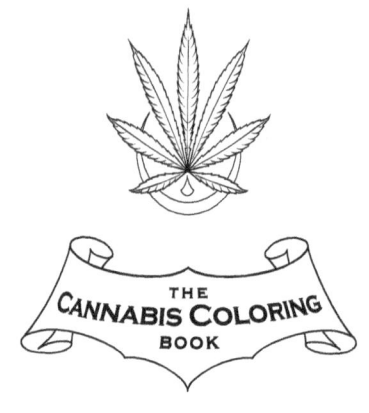

SECOND EDITION
2018

Indulge Creatively My Friends!

TO PURCHASE: **Retail:** bit.ly/FredGardner **Wholesale:** bit.ly/FGardner

Printed by CreateSpace, An Amazon.com Company

© FREDERICK GARDNER 2017

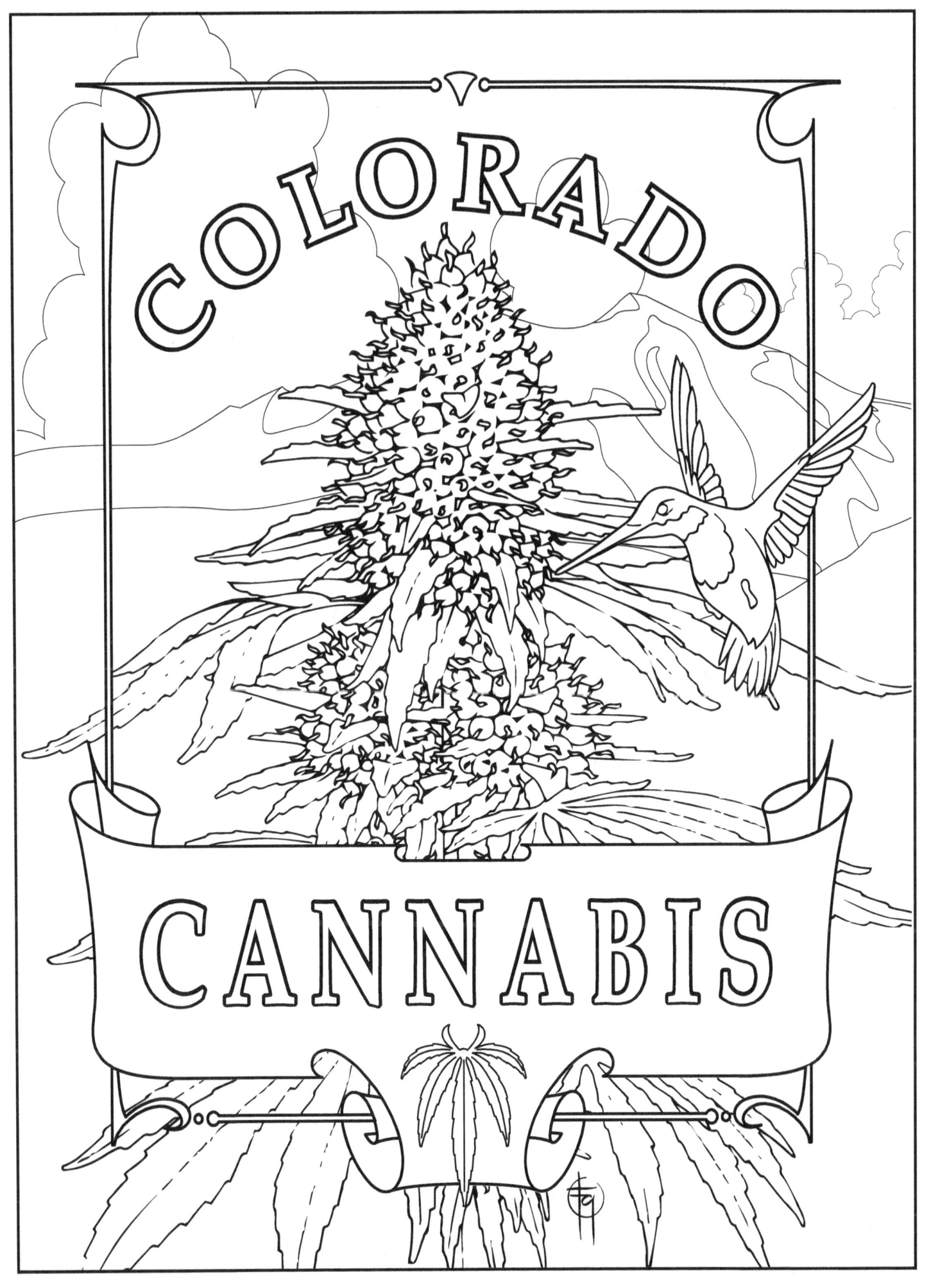

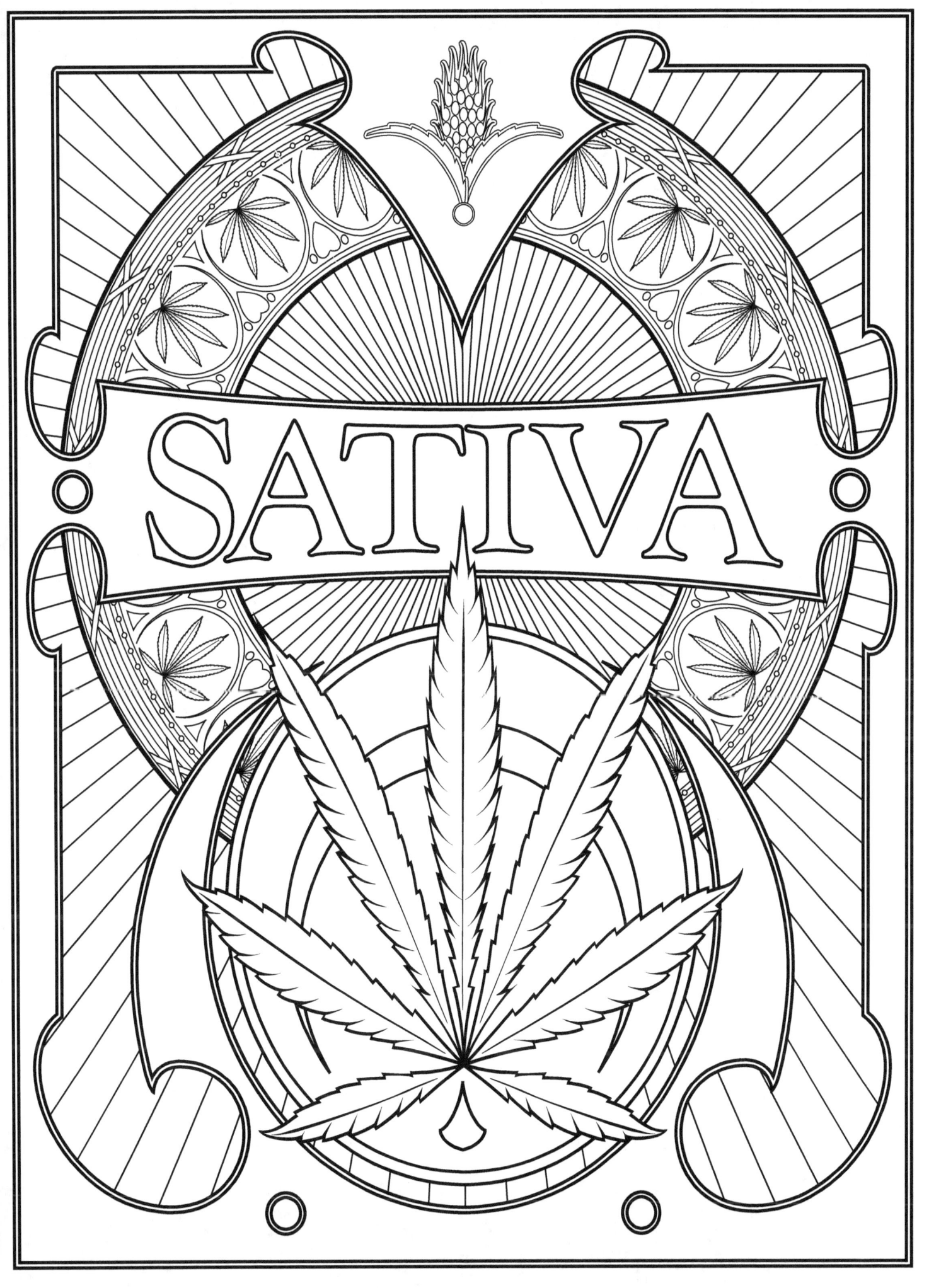

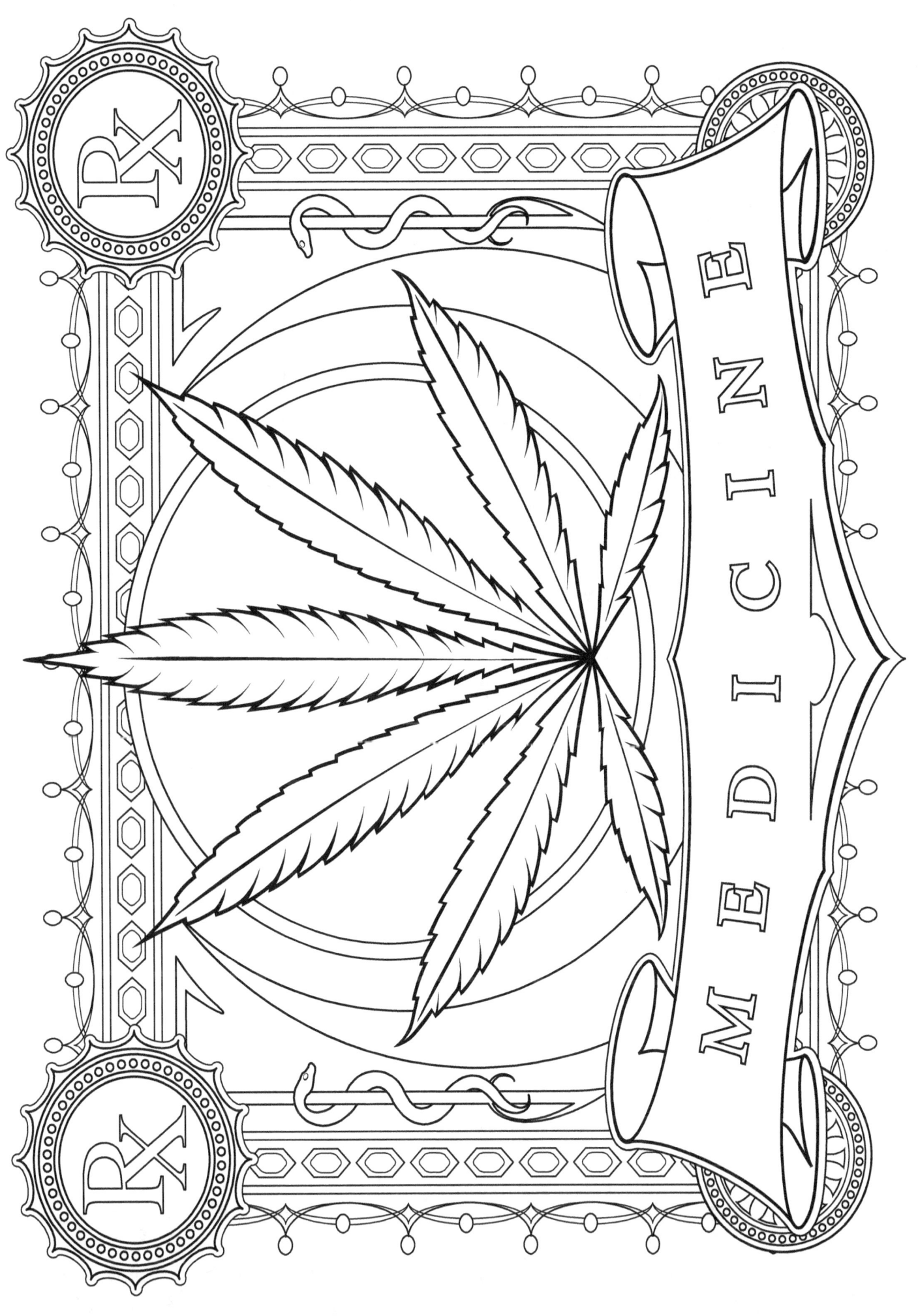

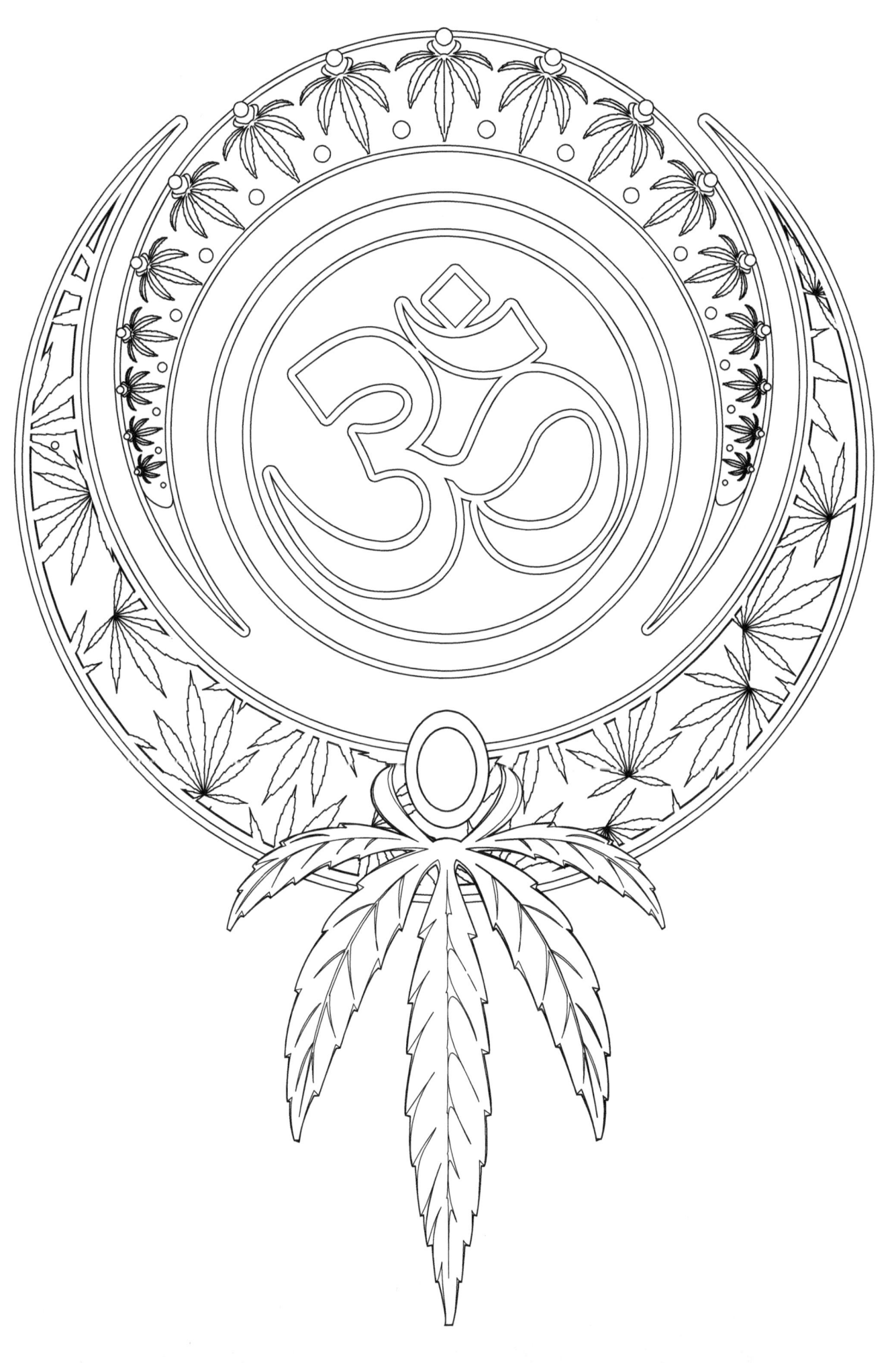

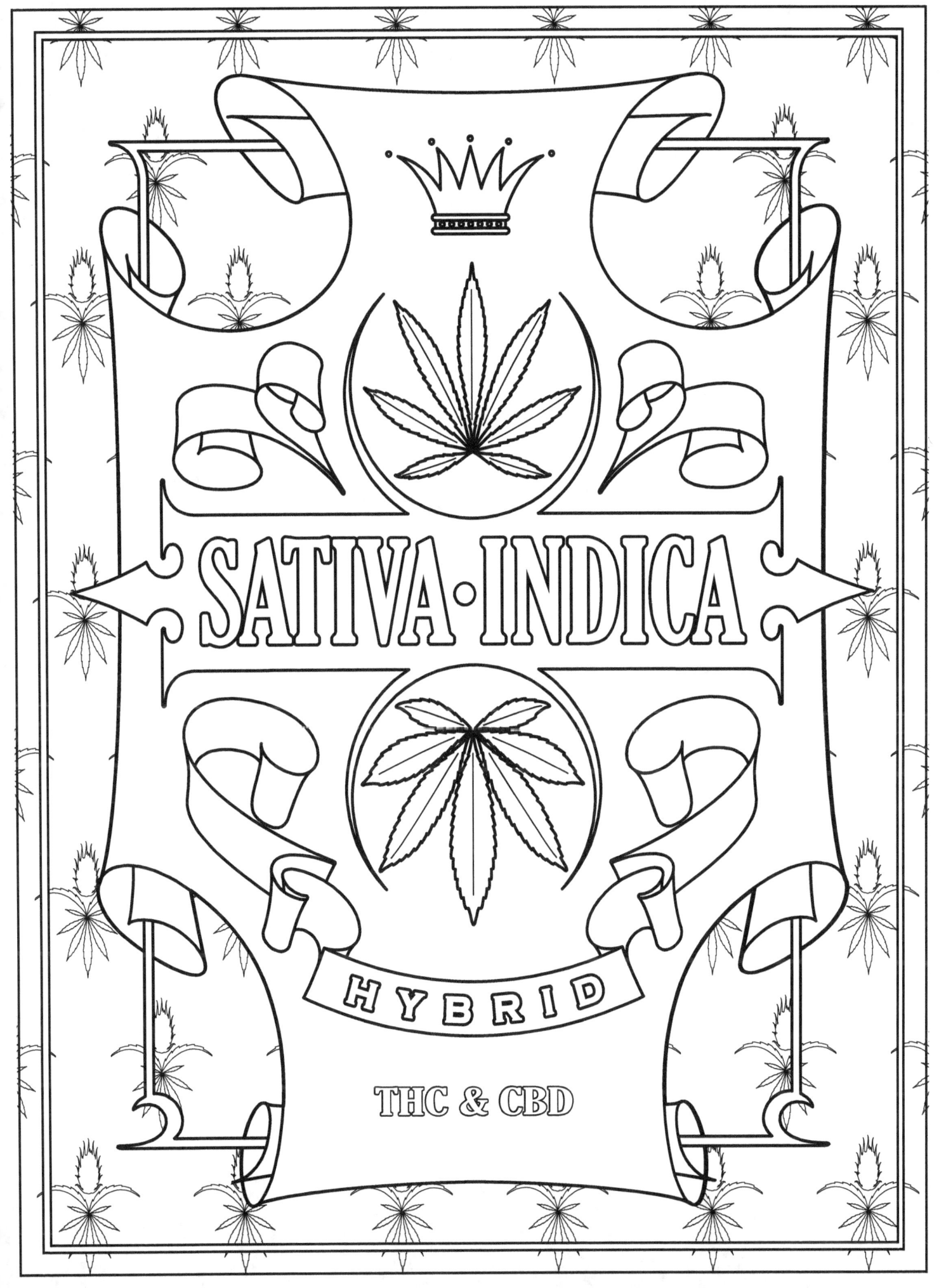

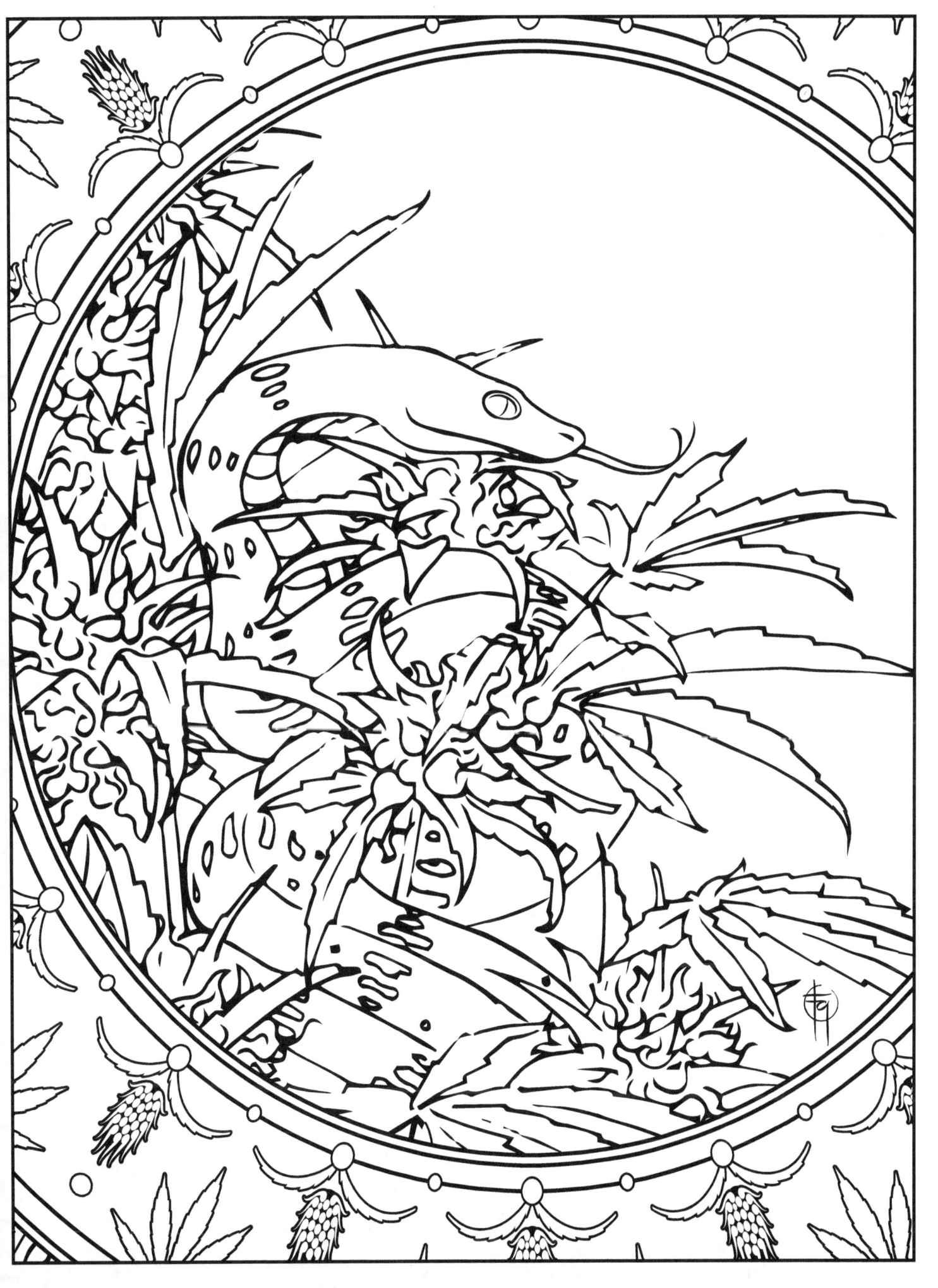

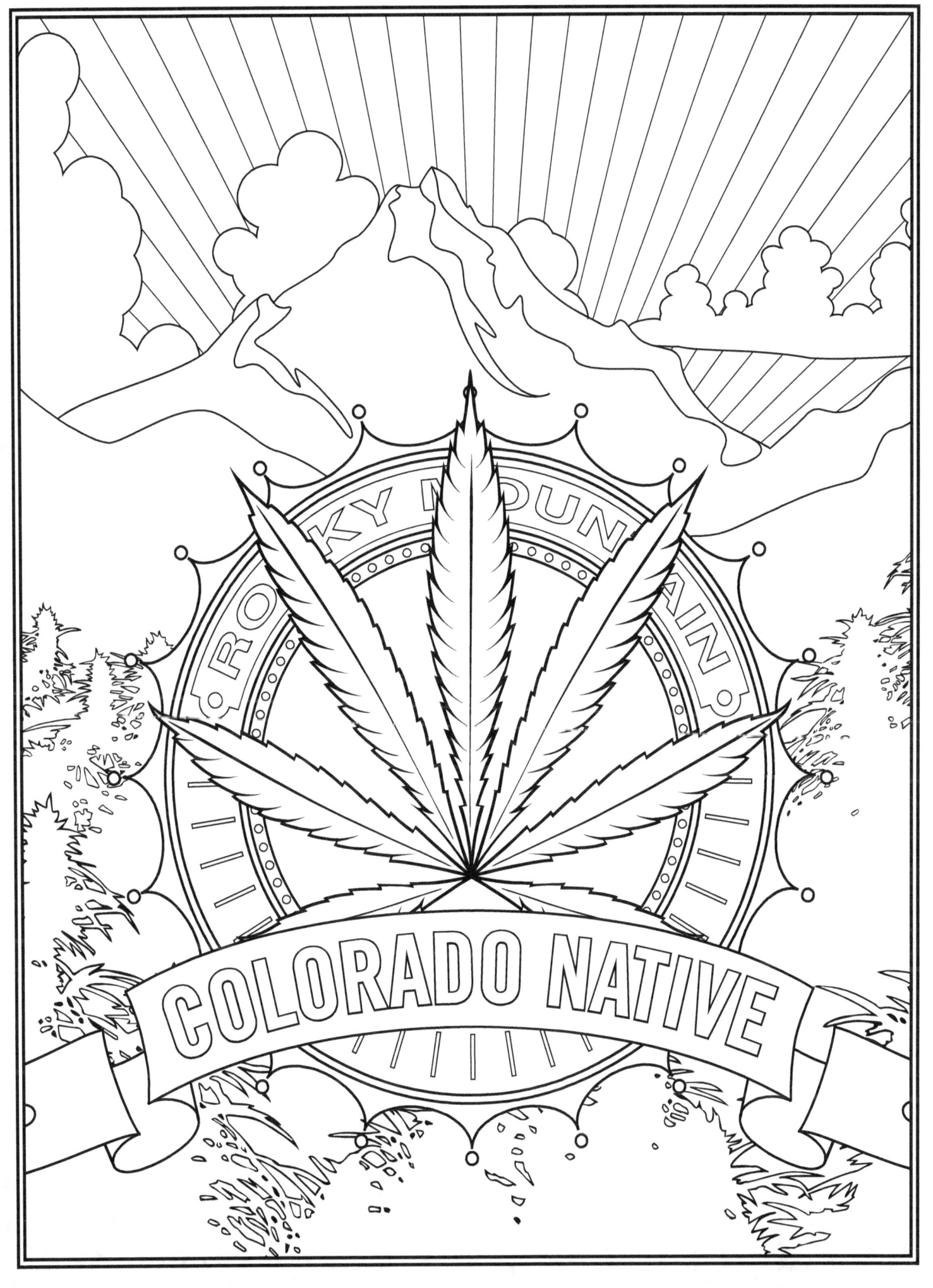

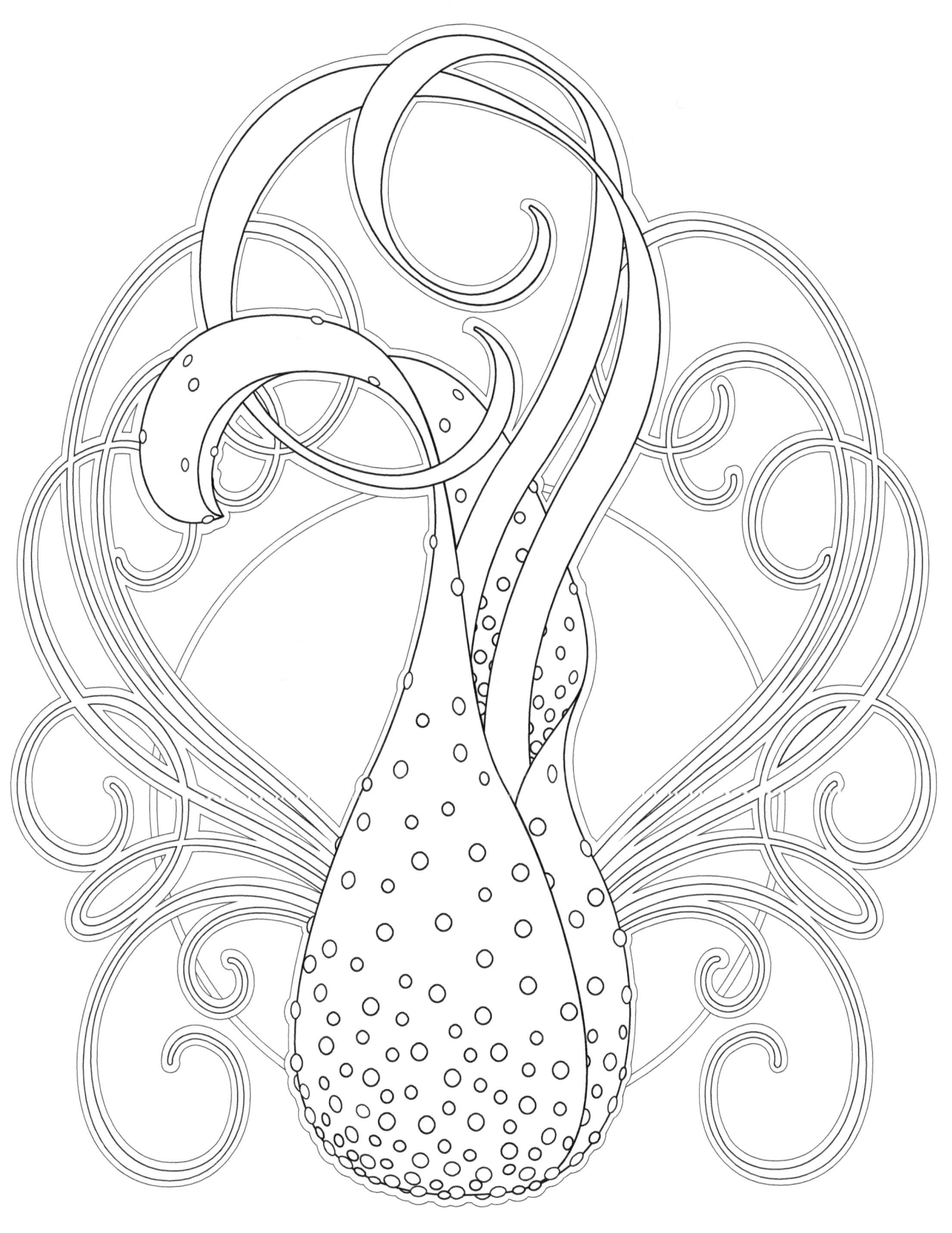

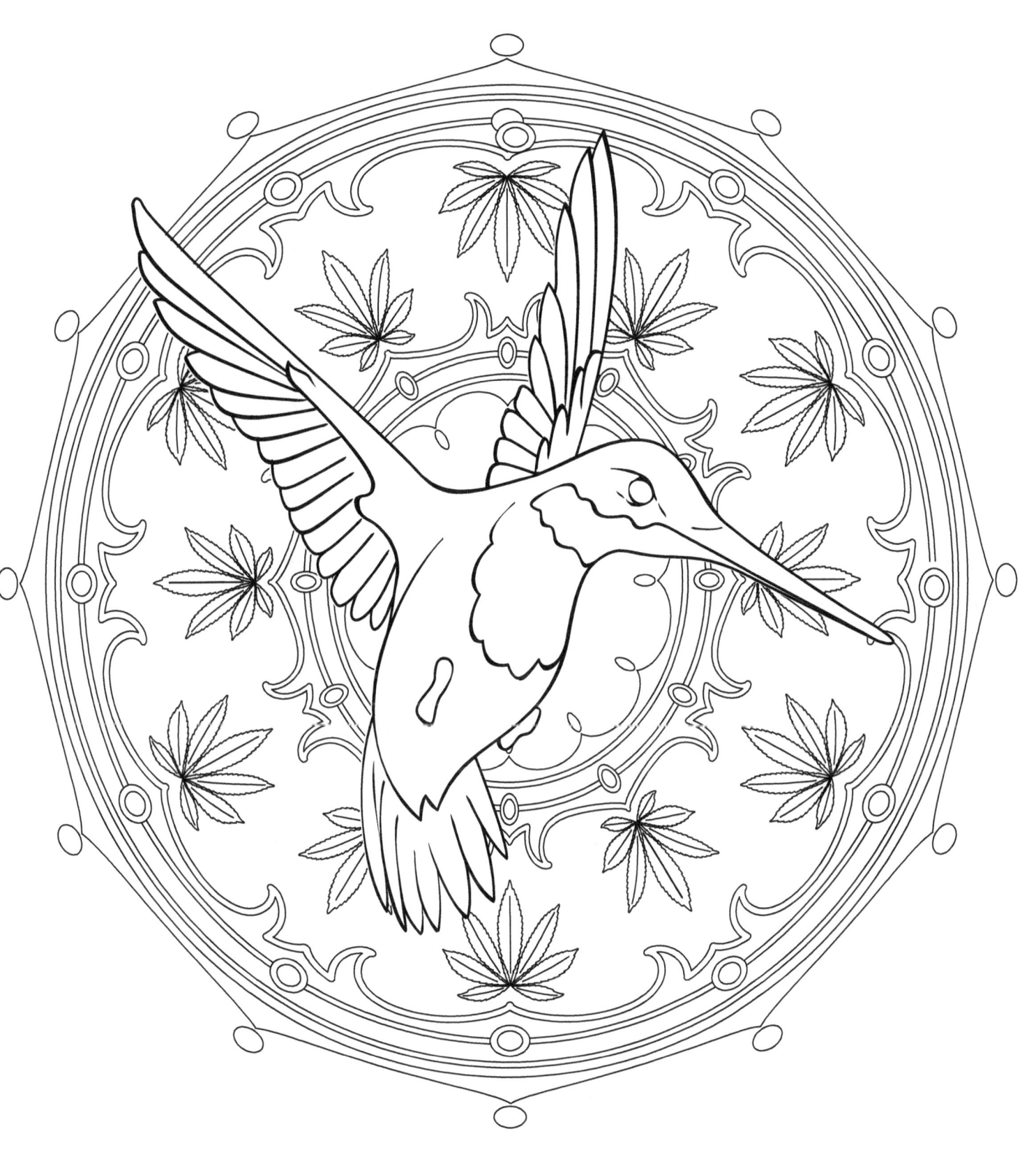

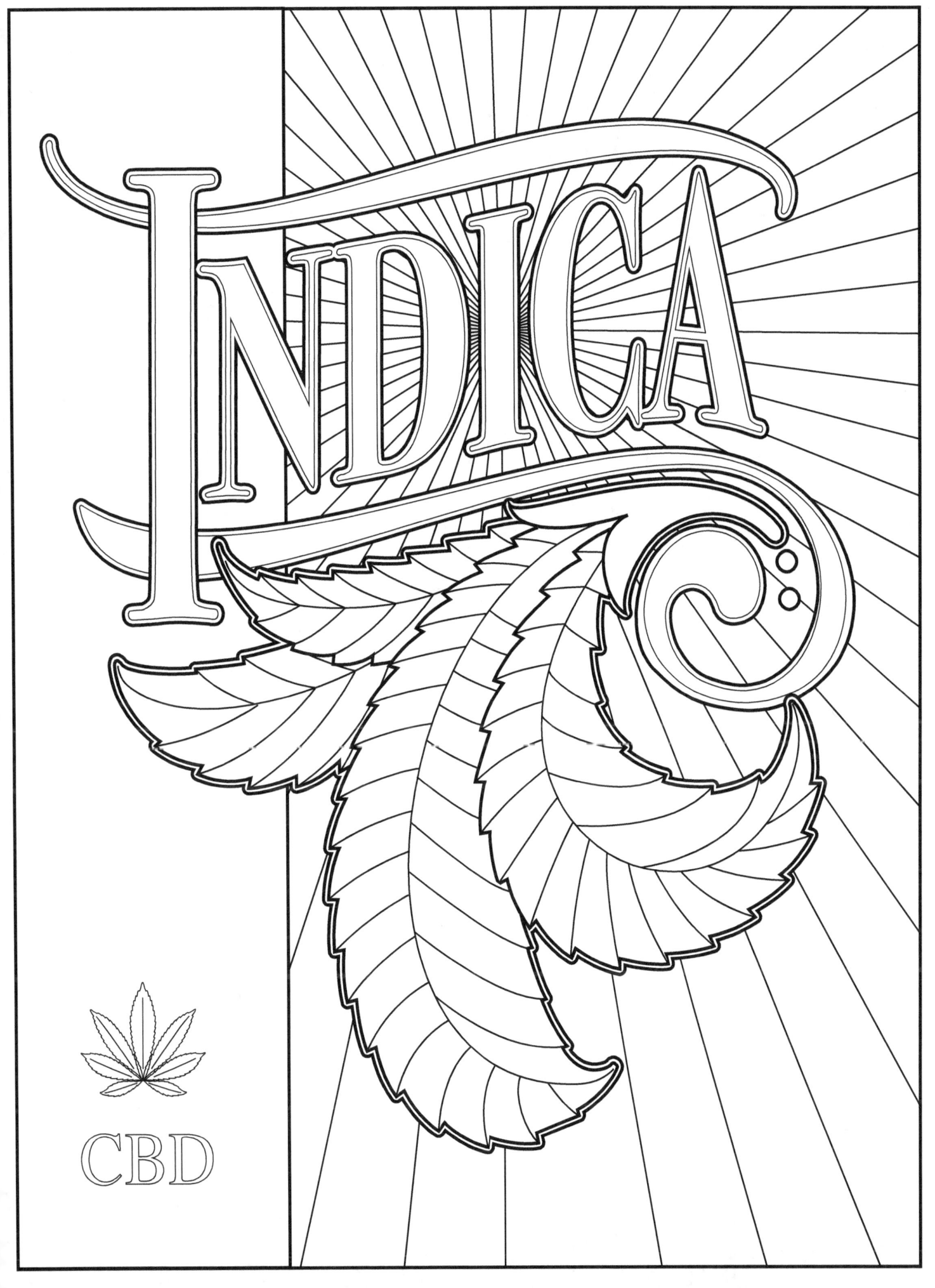

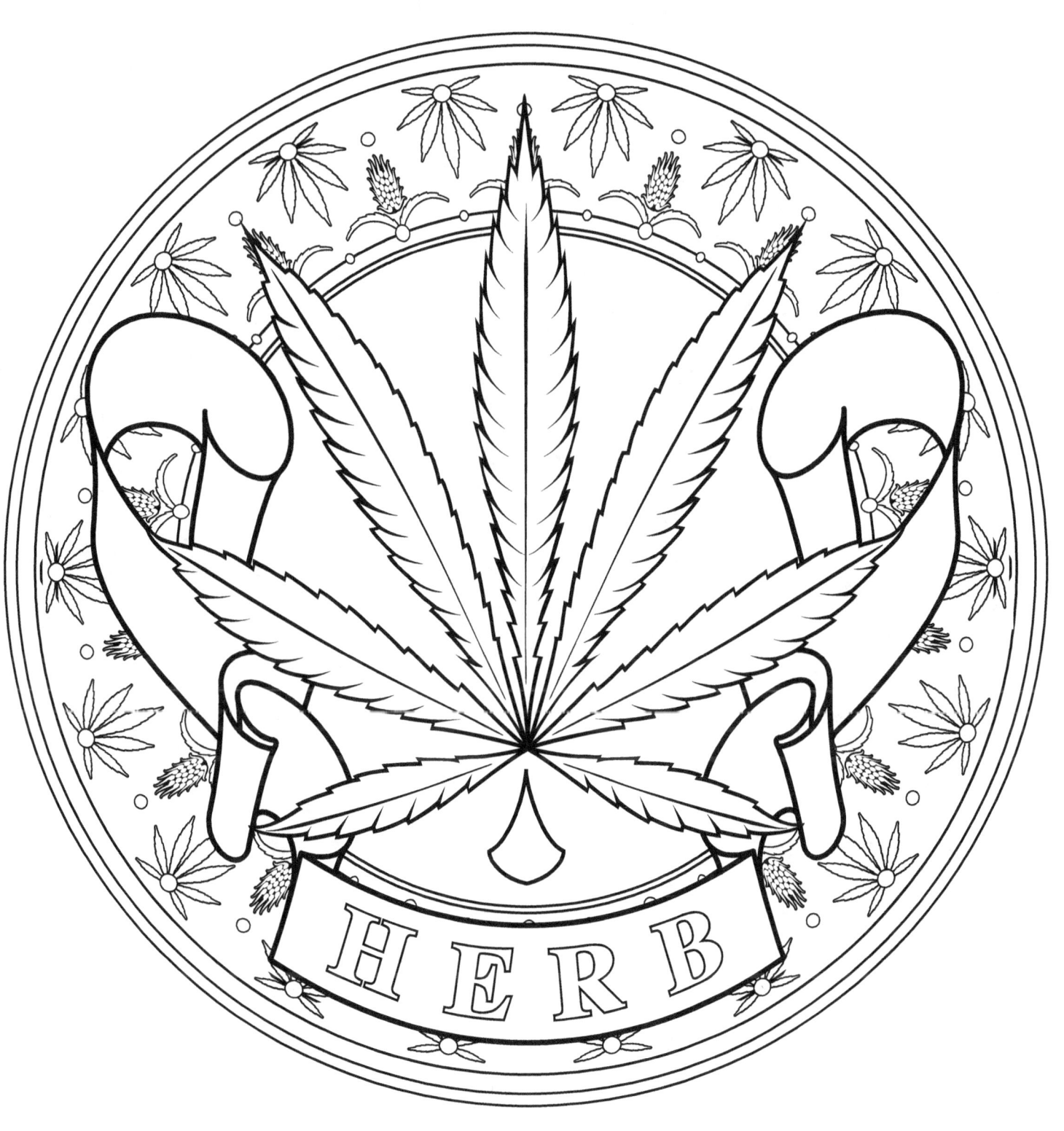

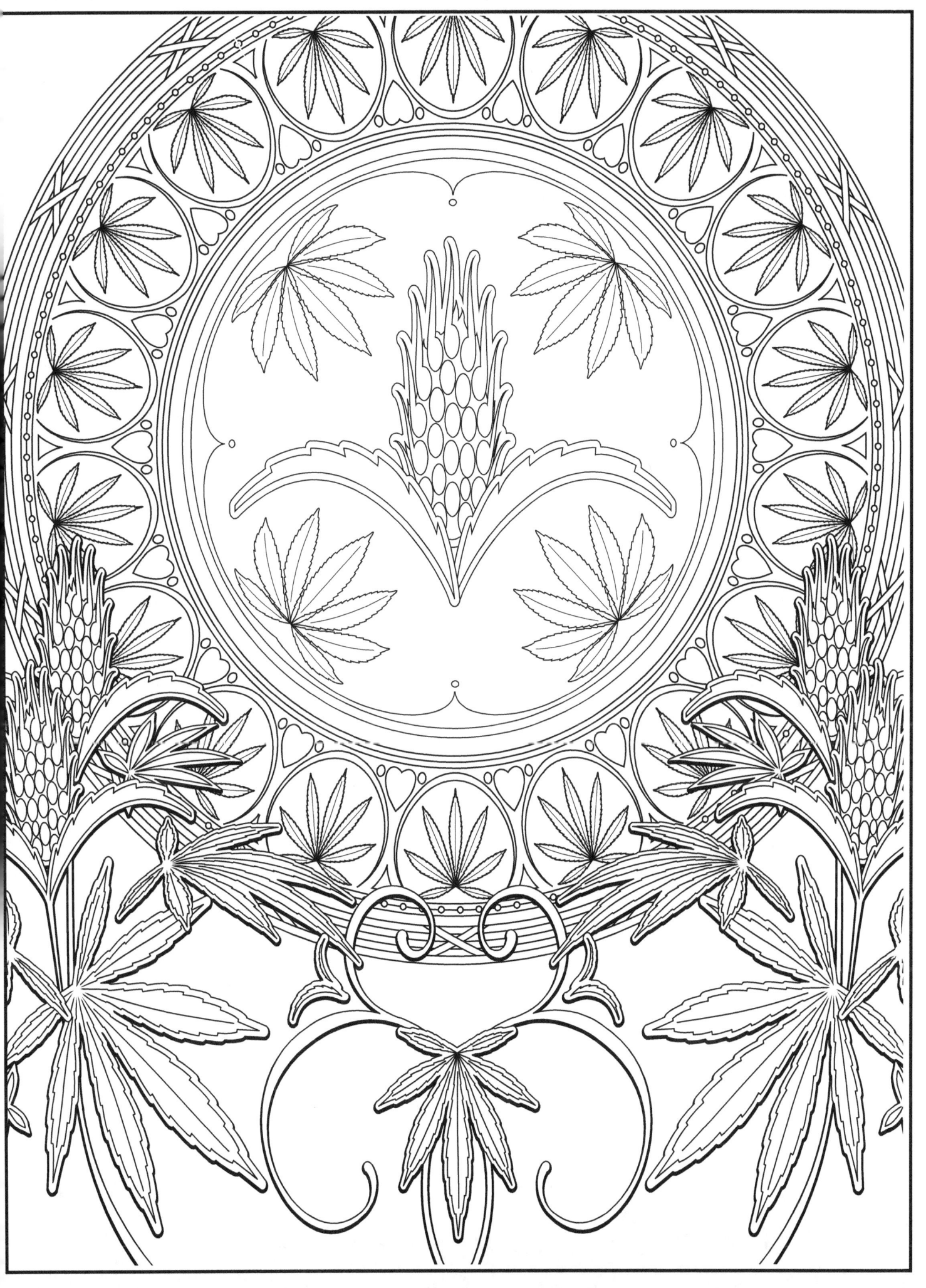

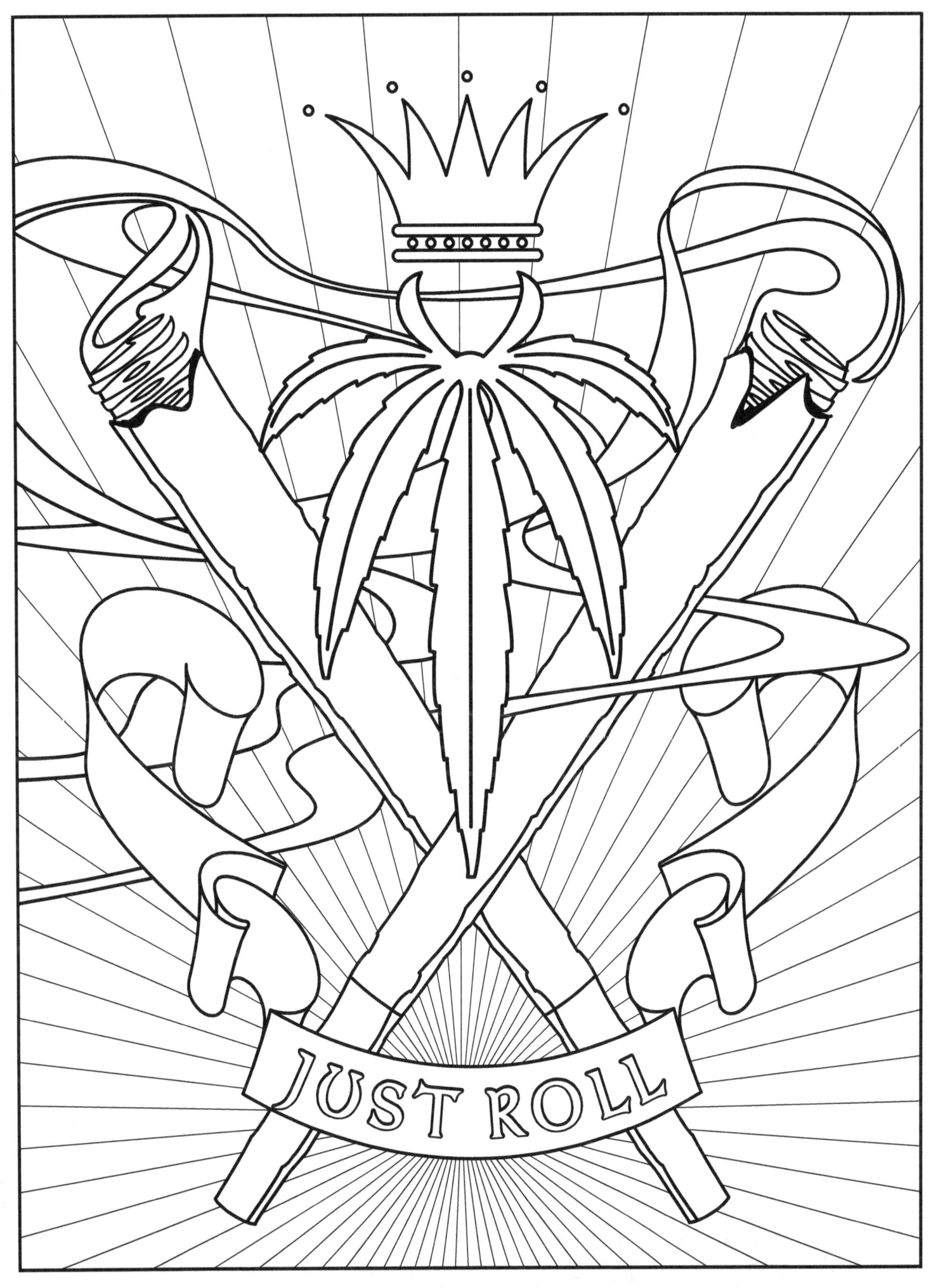

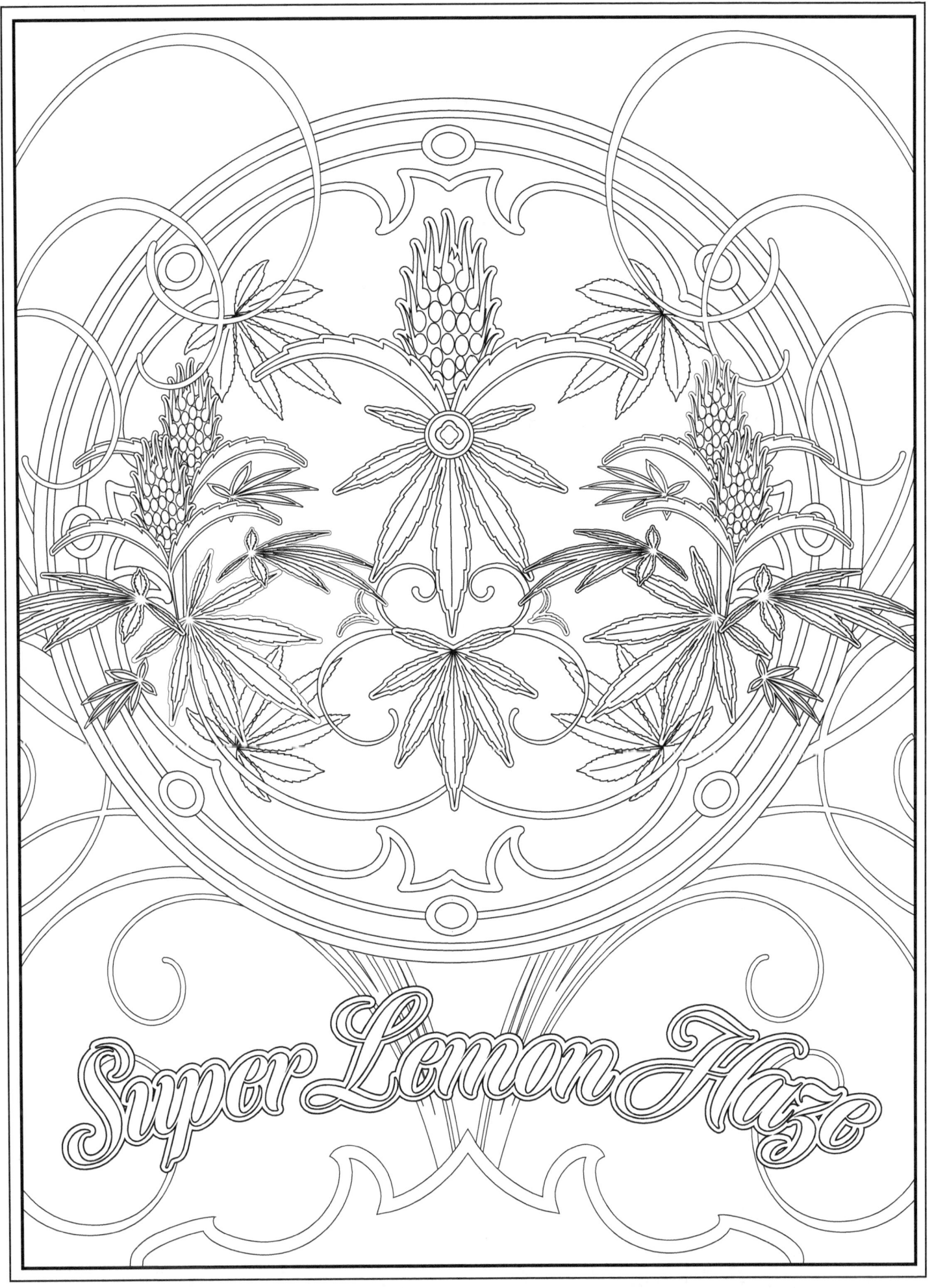

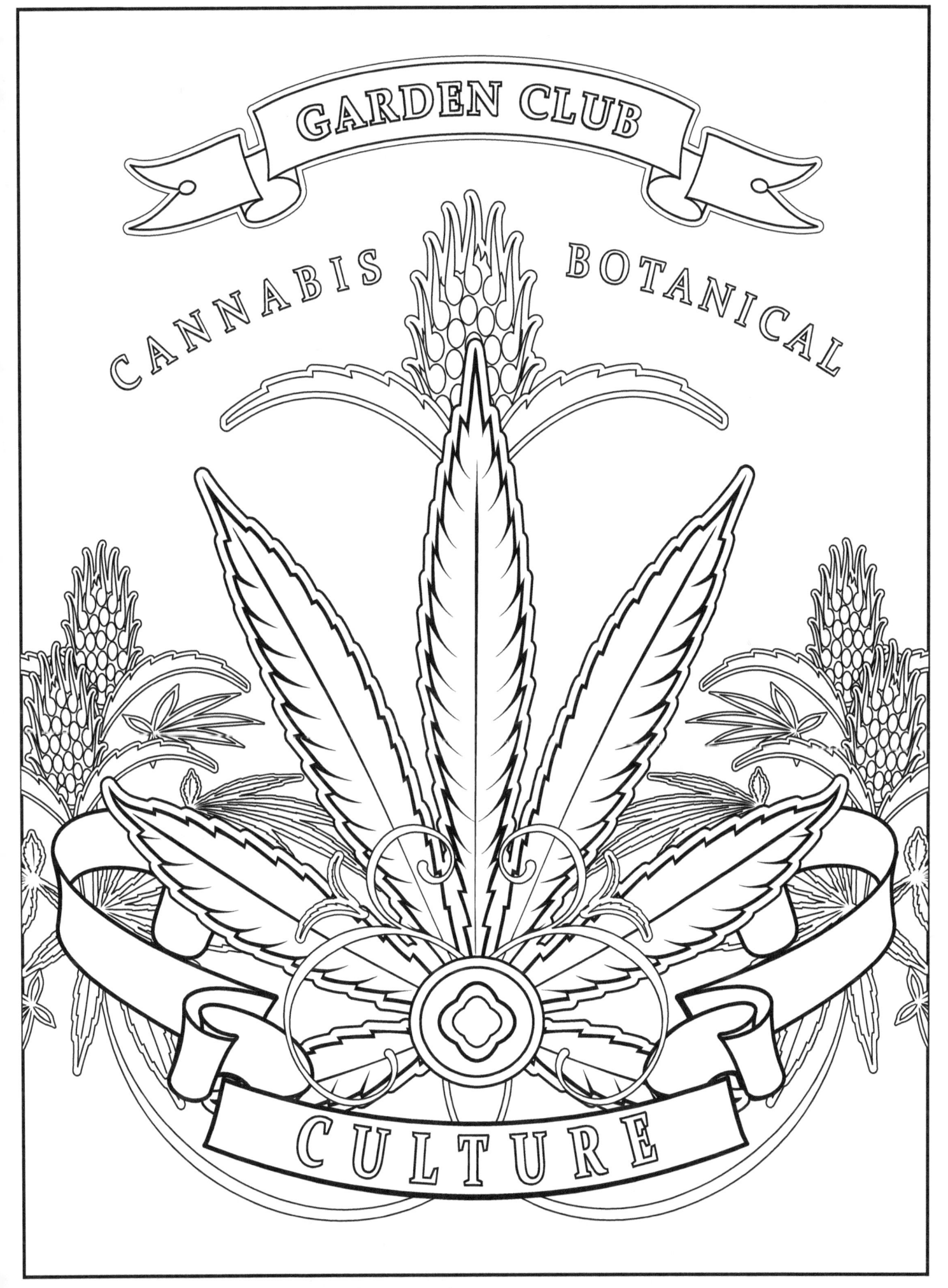

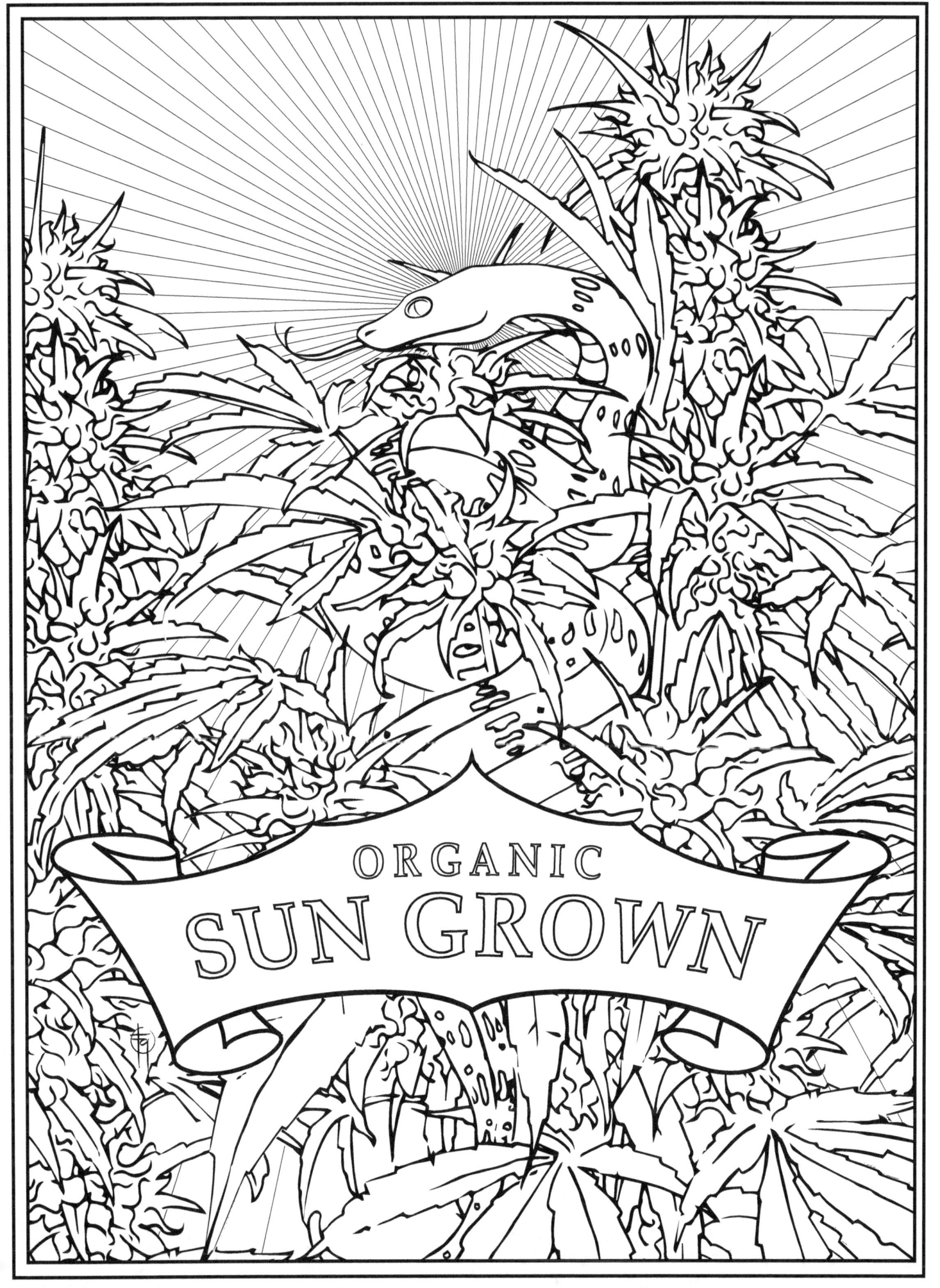

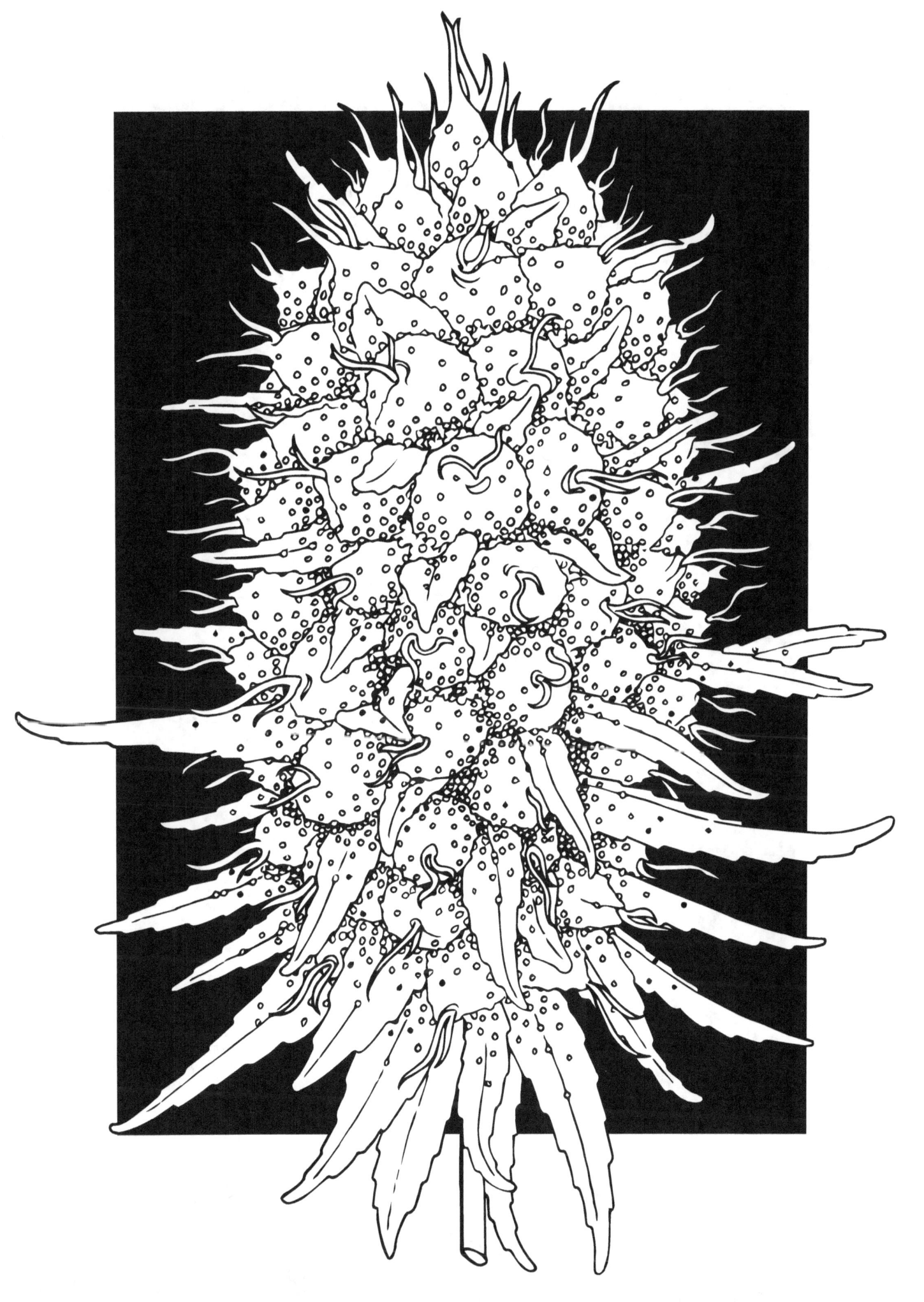

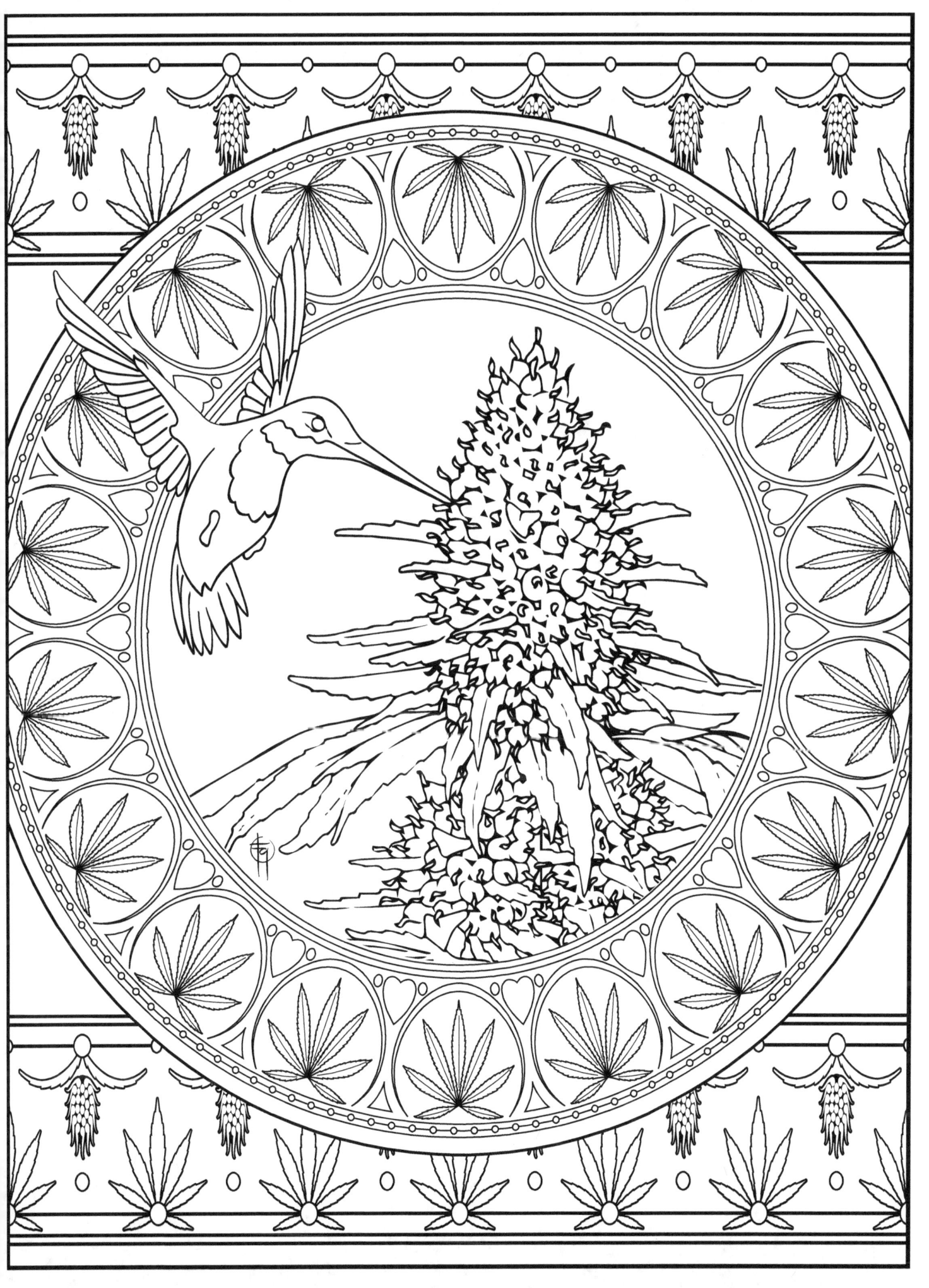

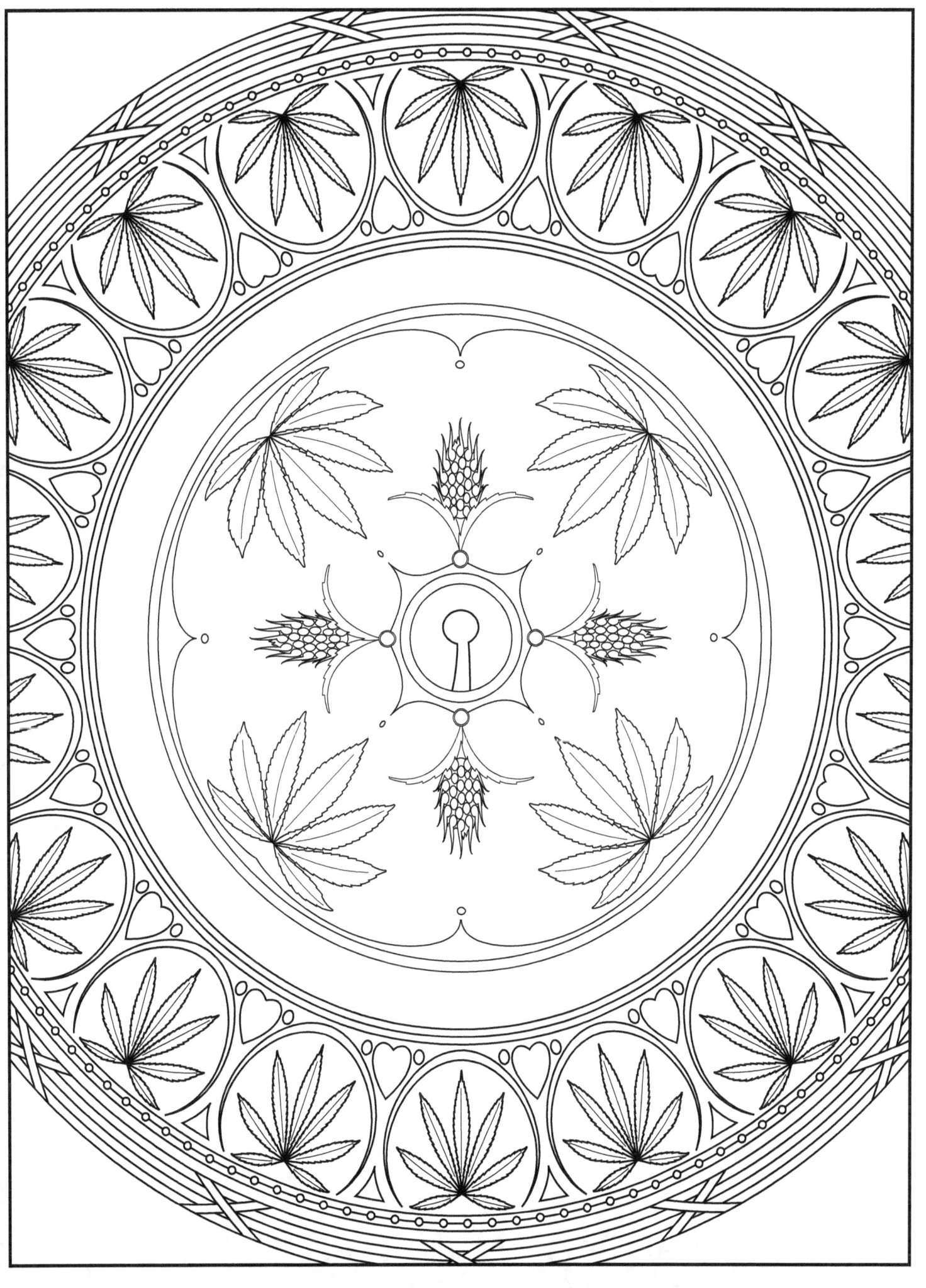

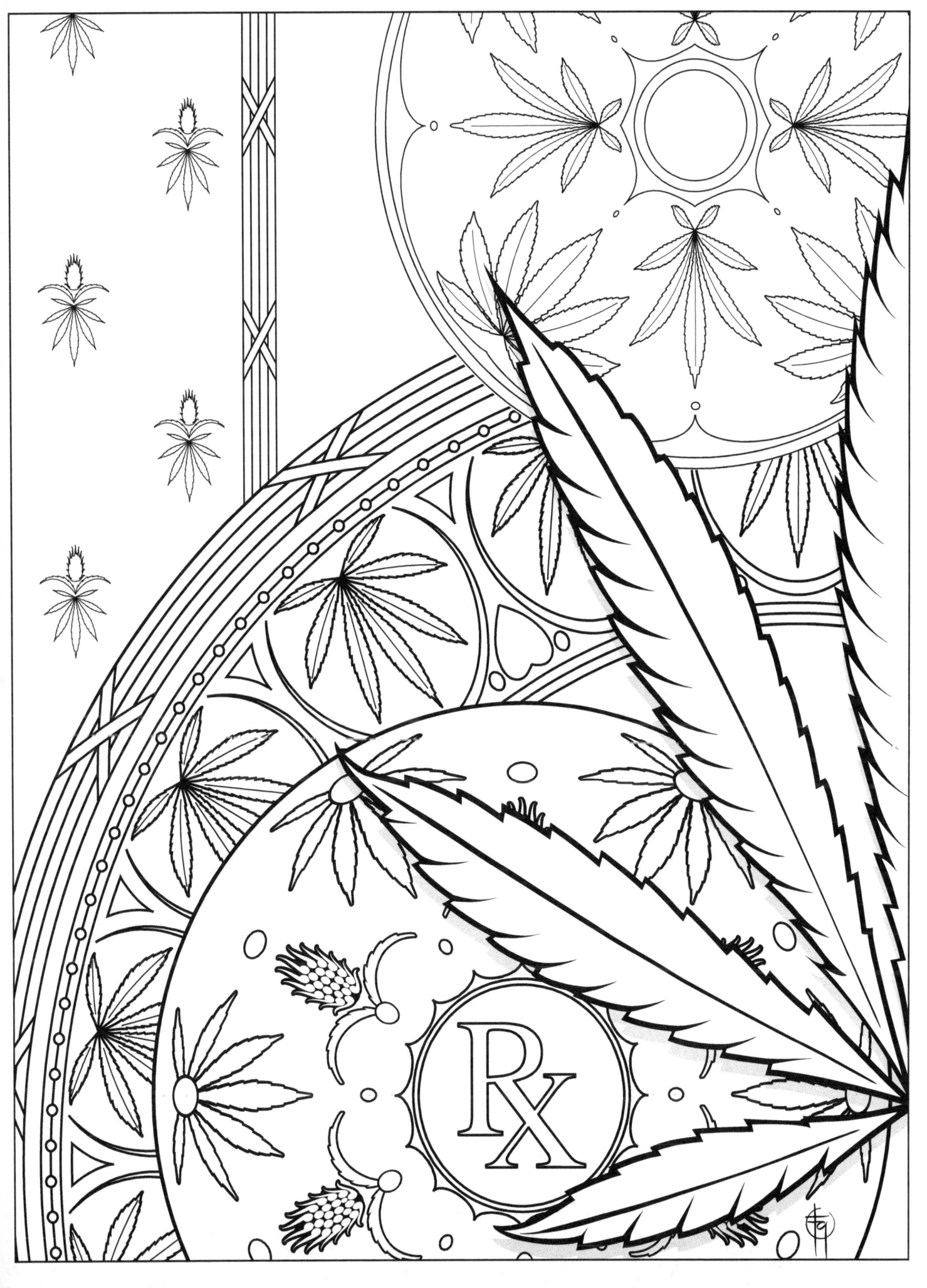

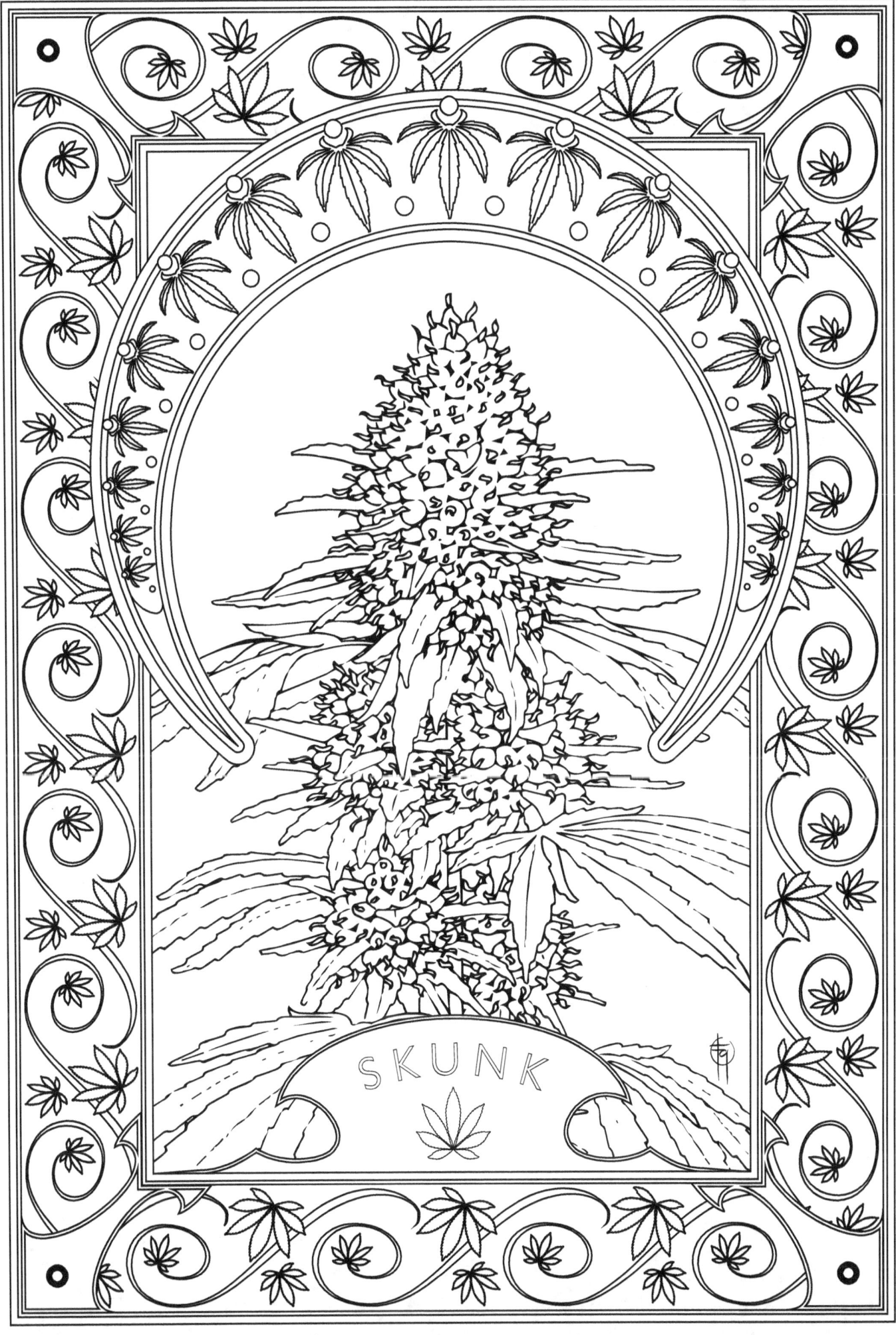

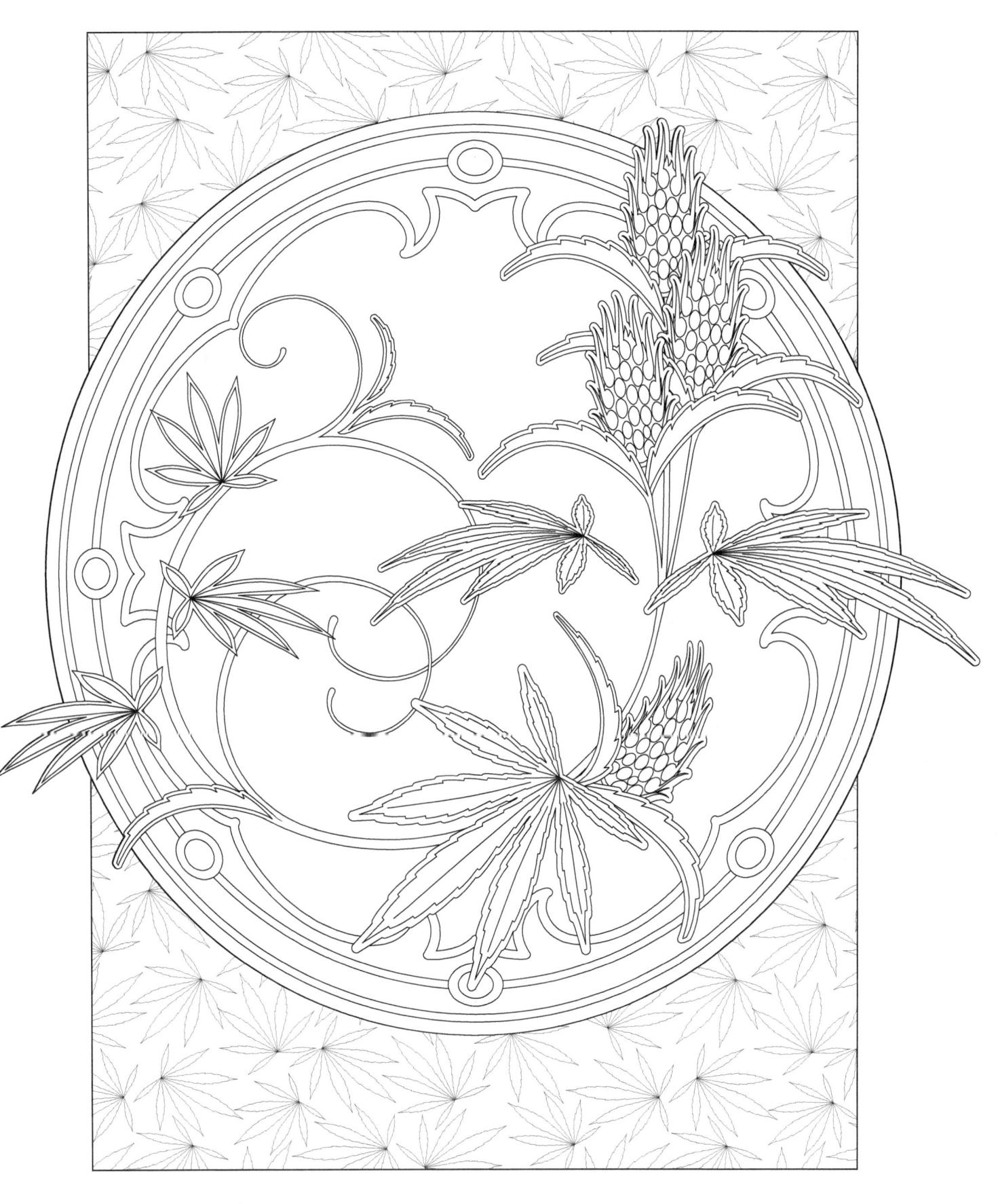

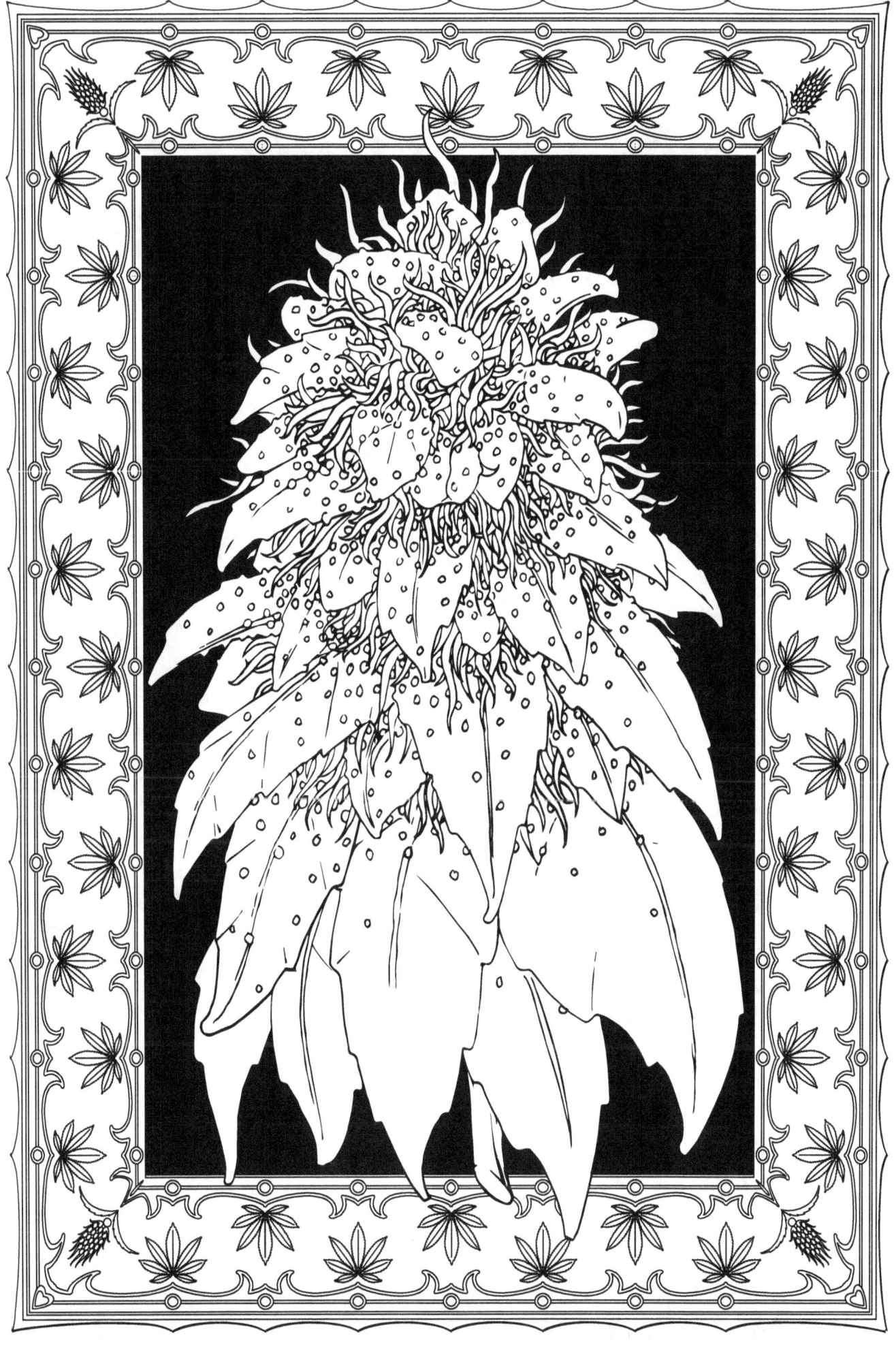

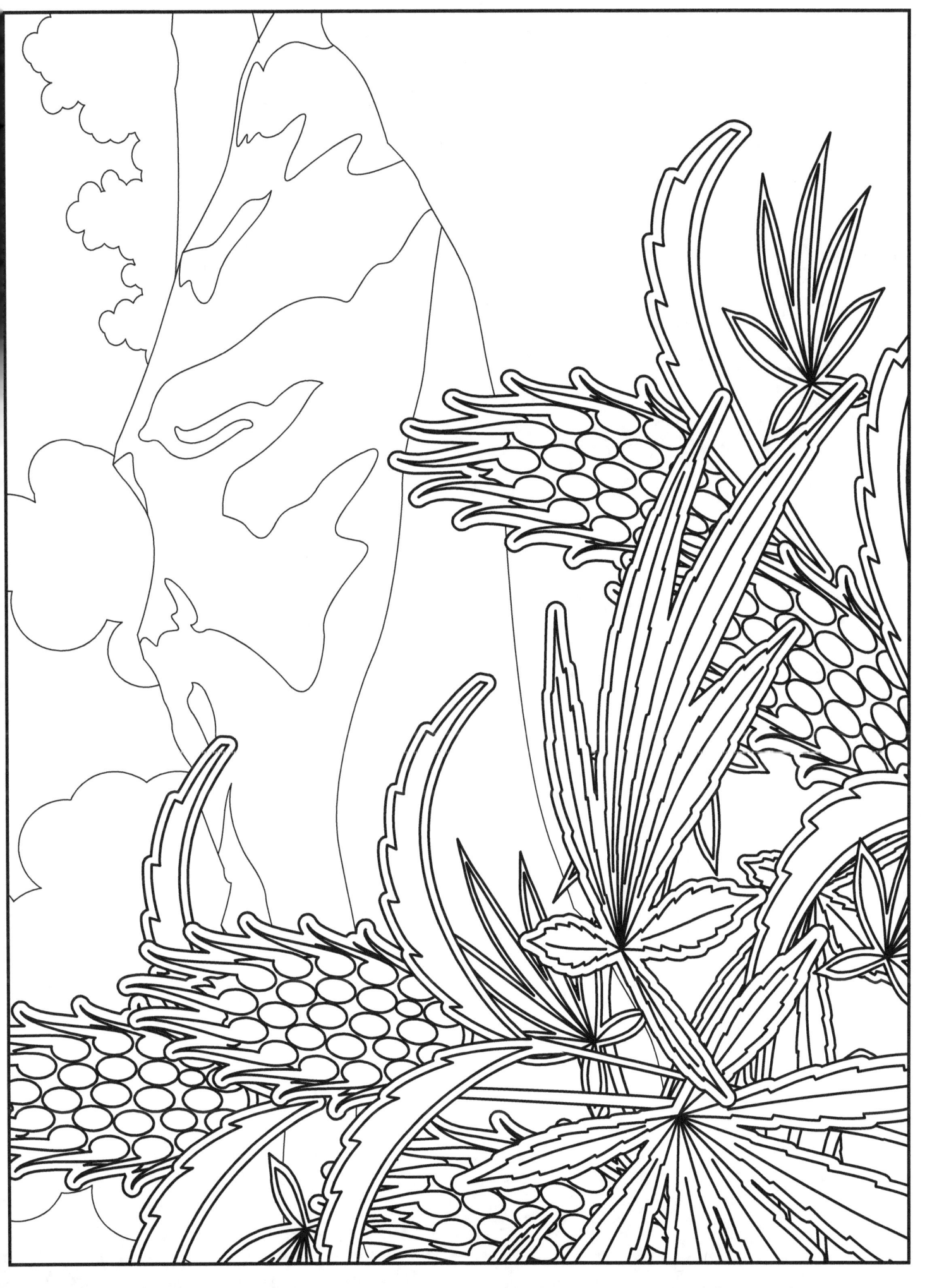

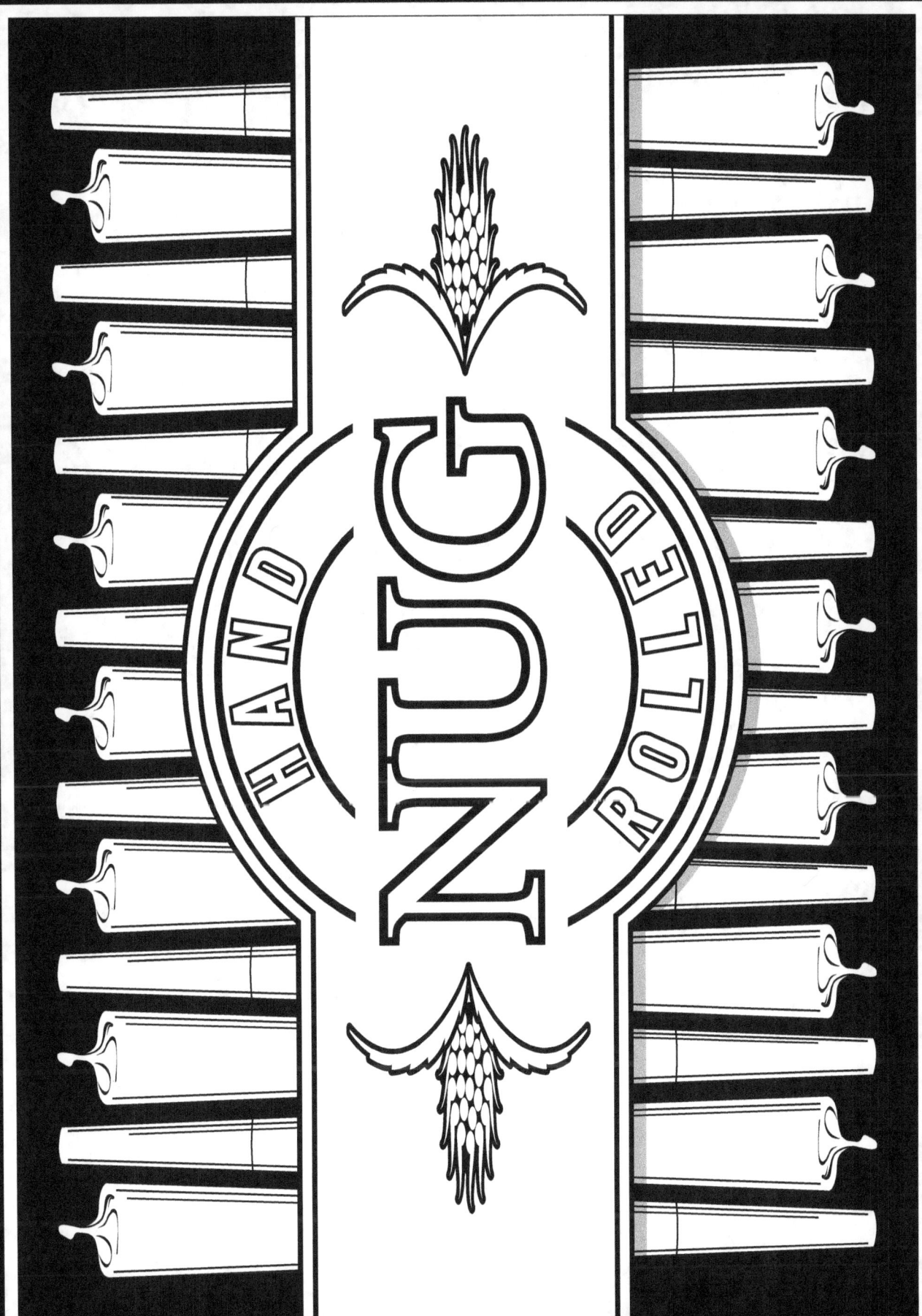

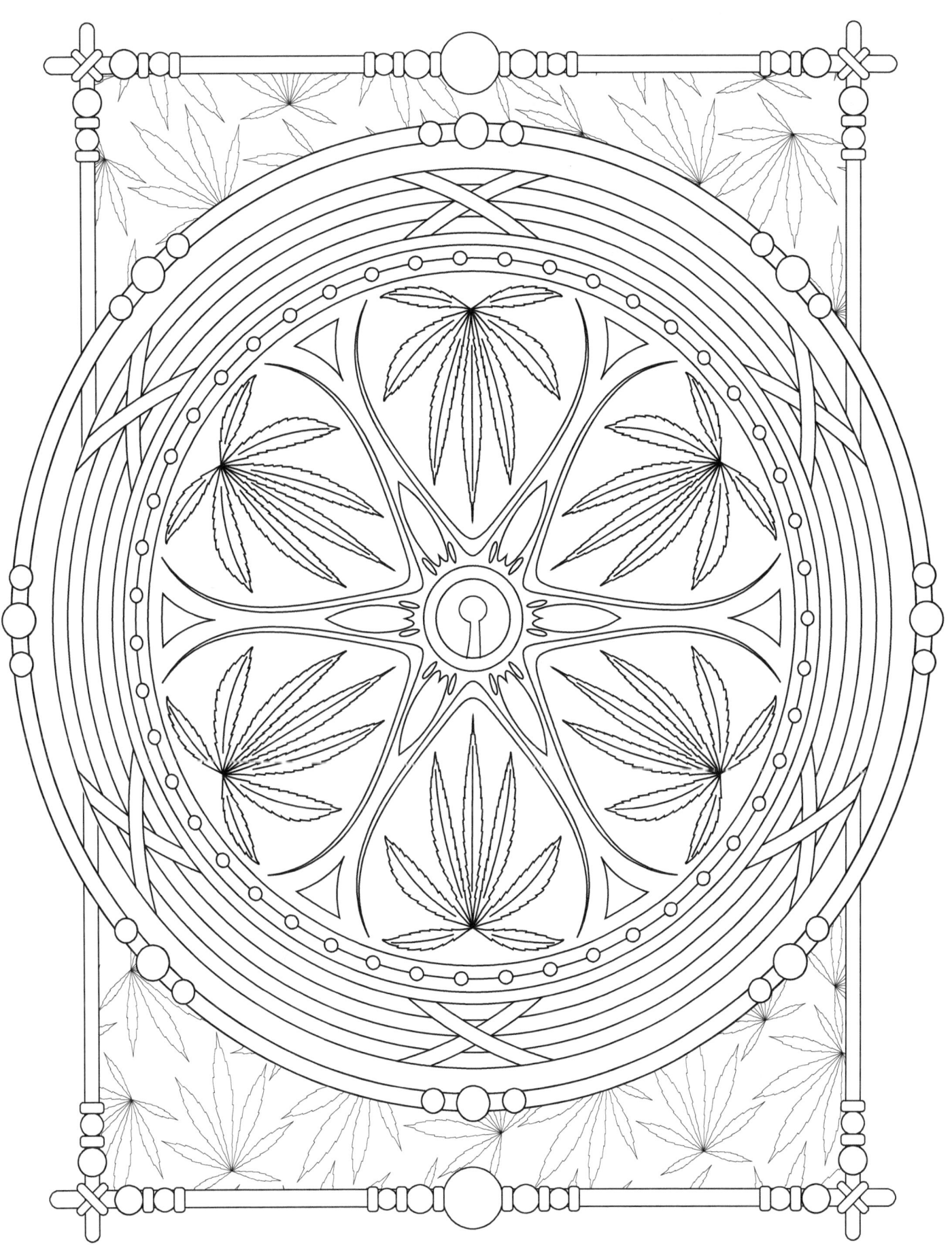

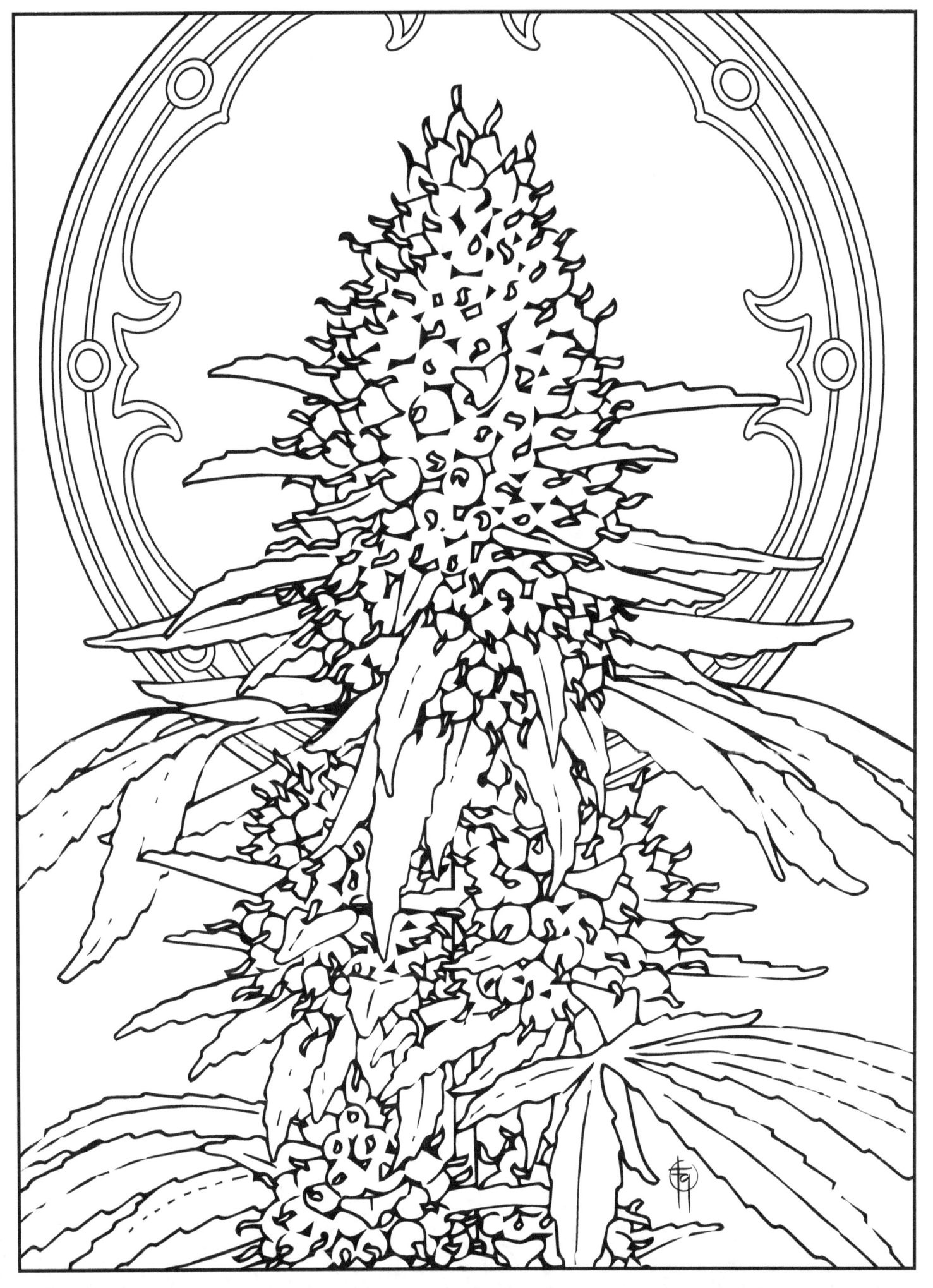

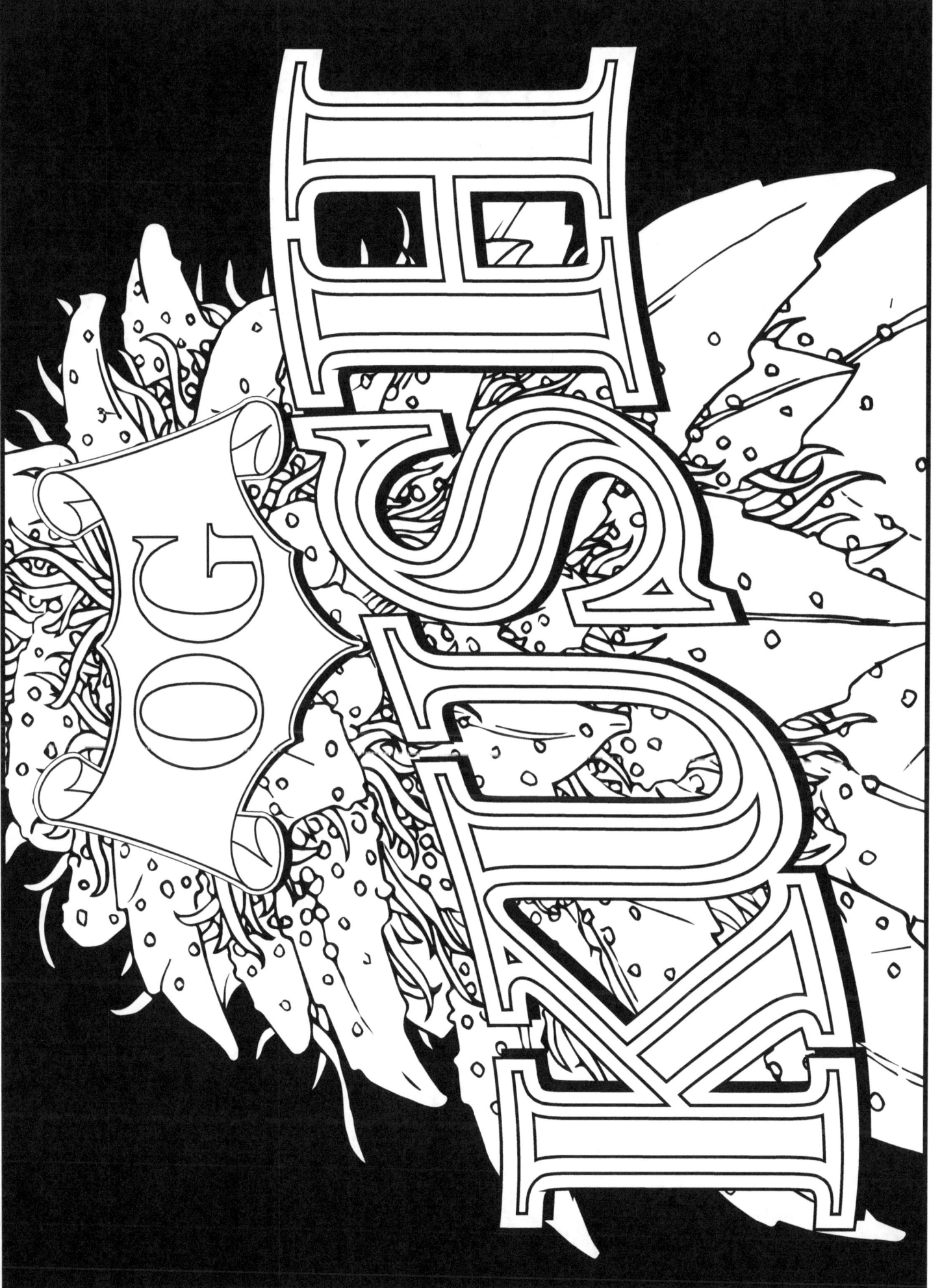

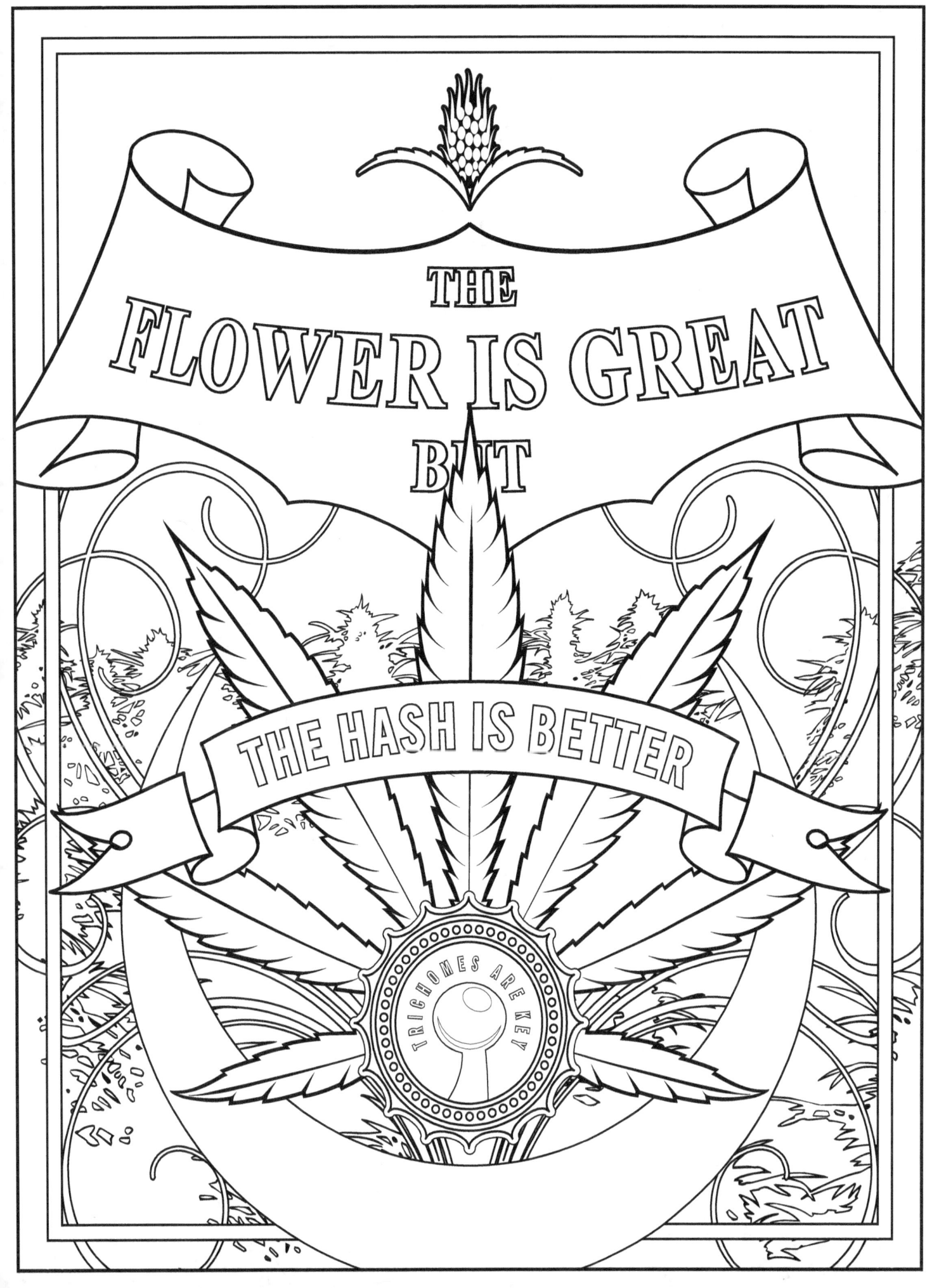

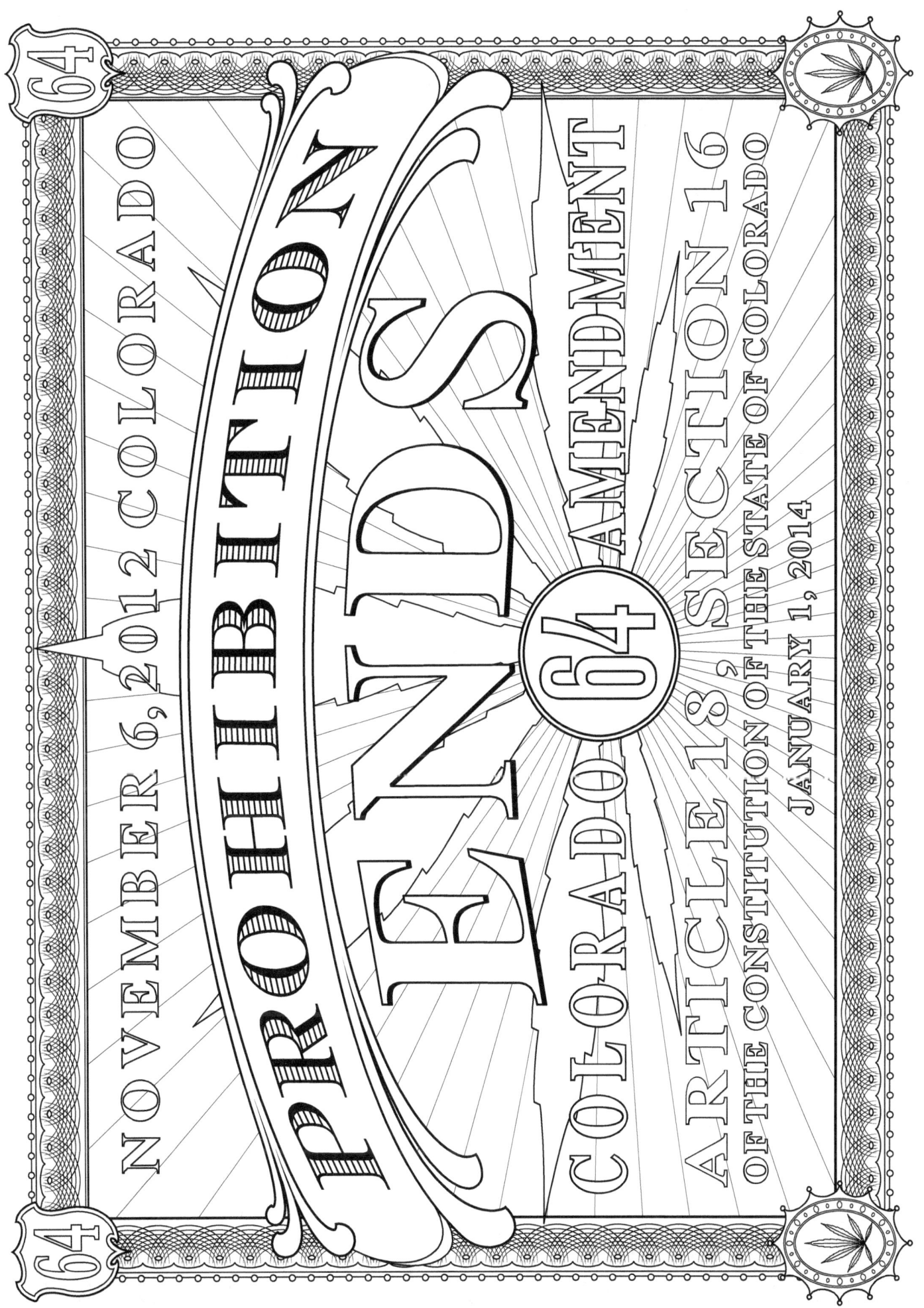

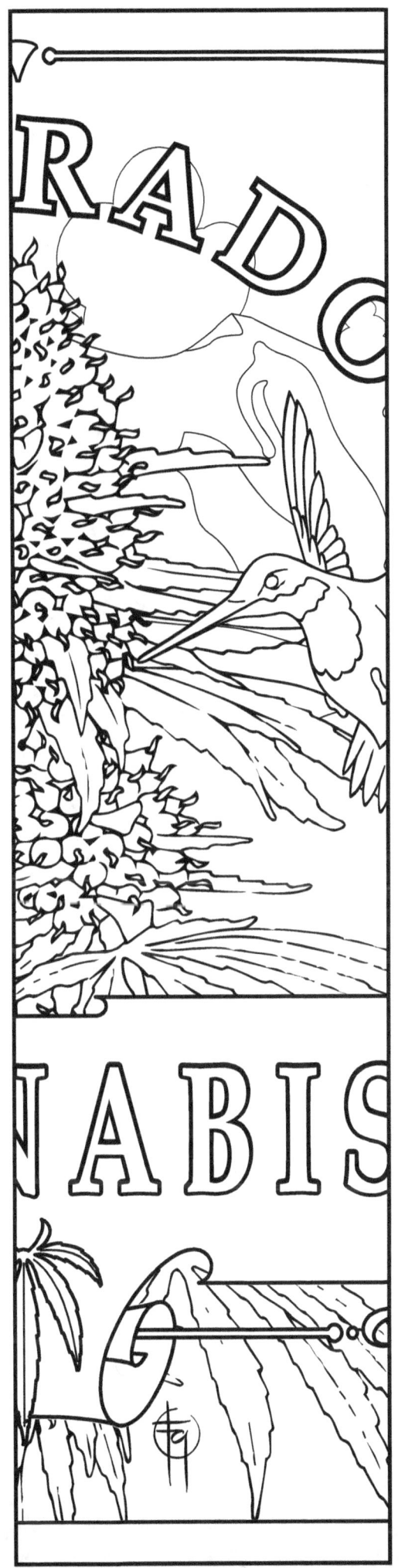

COLOR STUDY STRIPS

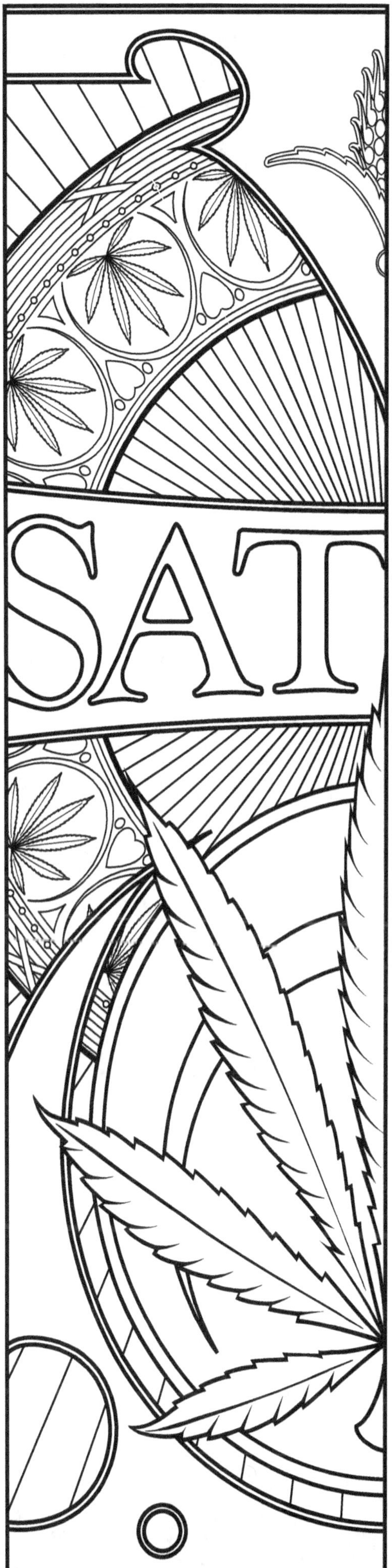

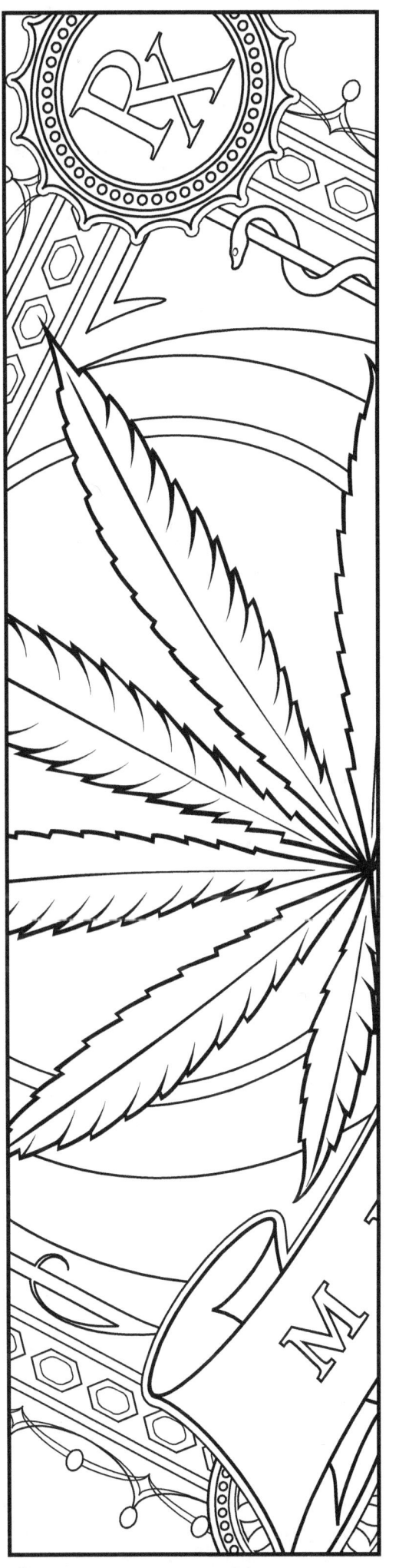
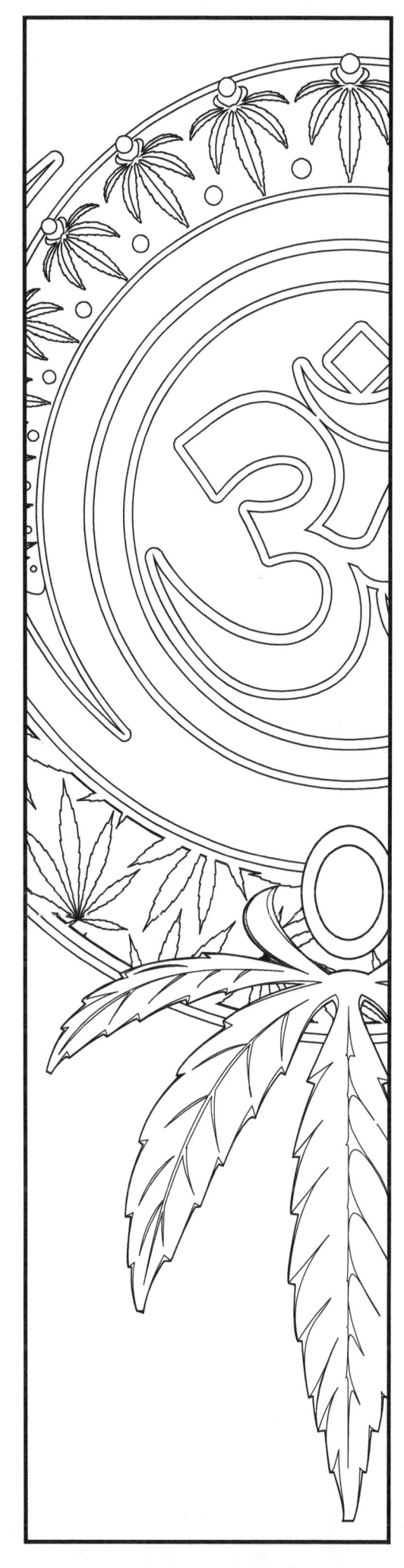

COLOR STUDY STRIPS

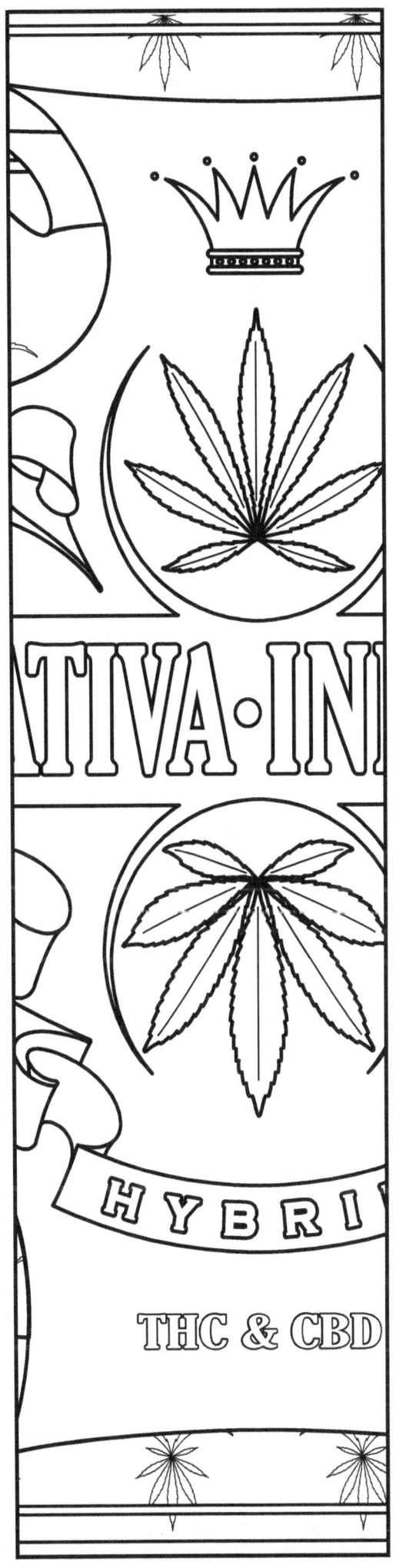

COLOR STUDY STRIPS

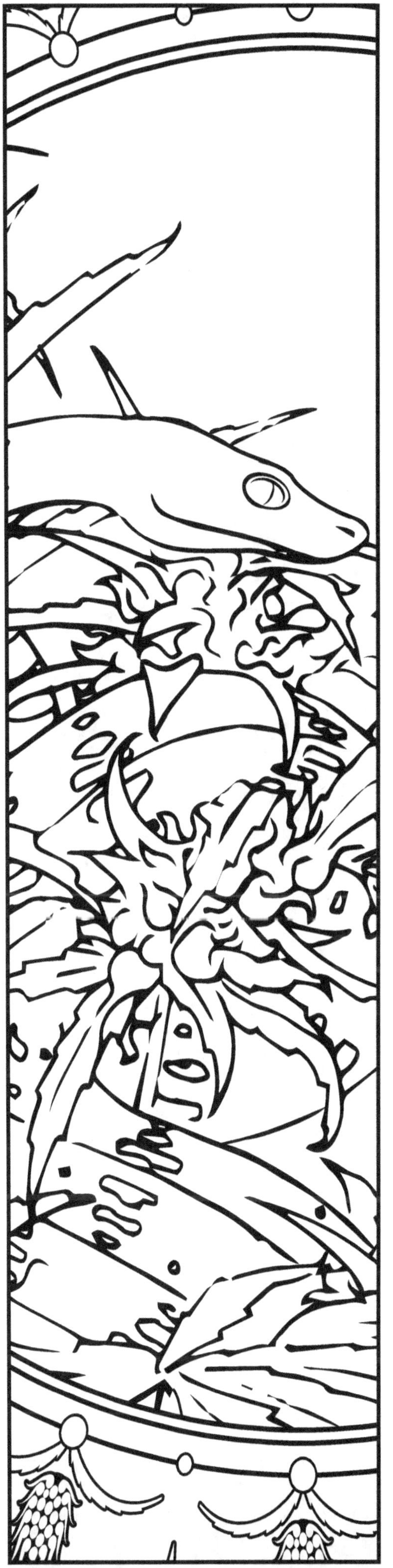

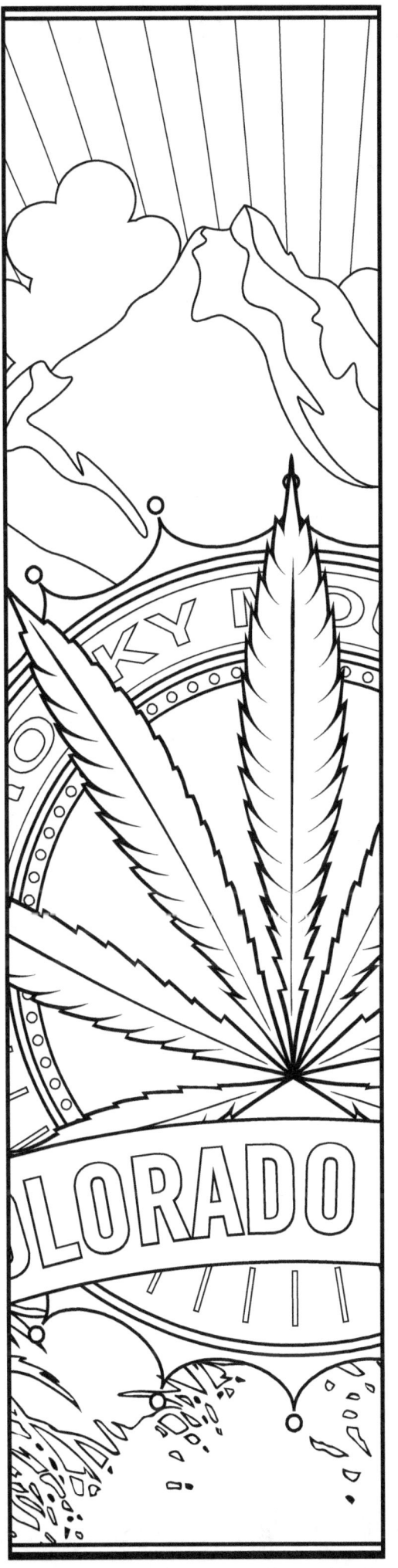 COLOR STUDY STRIPS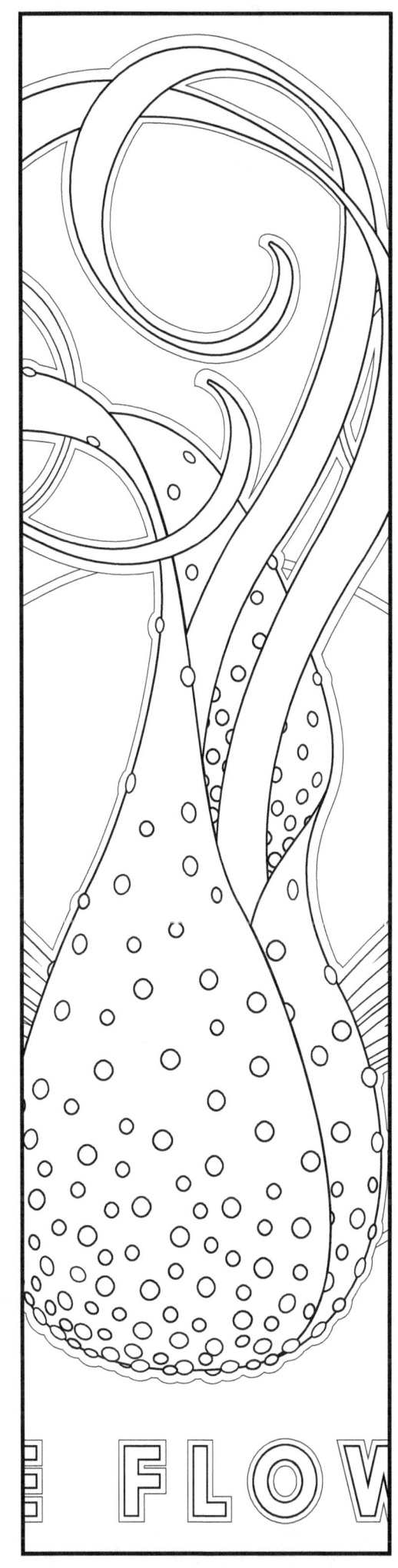

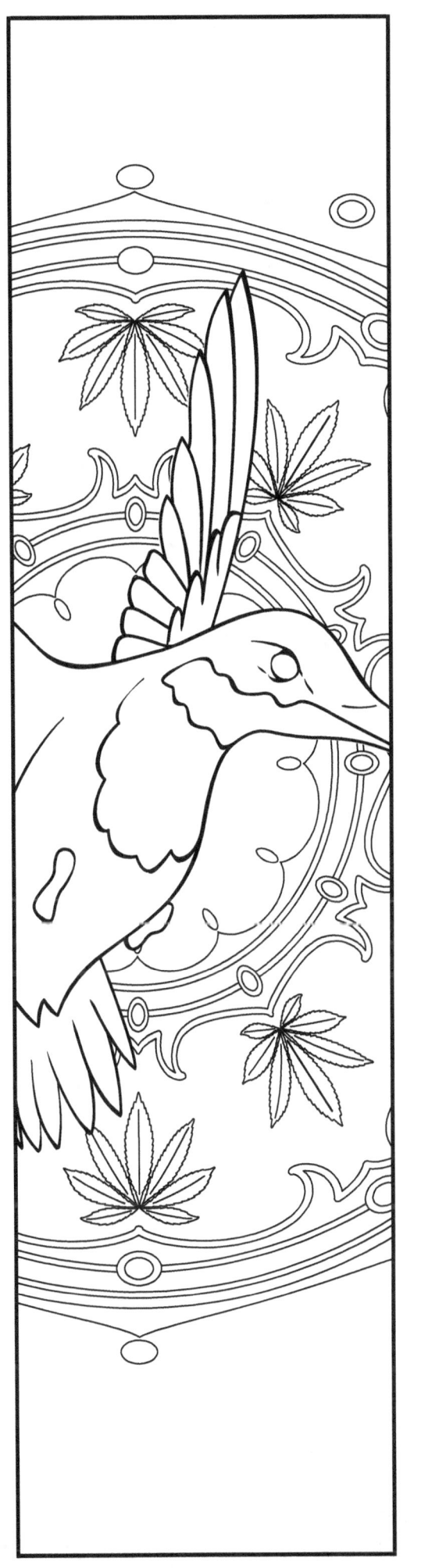

COLOR STUDY STRIPS

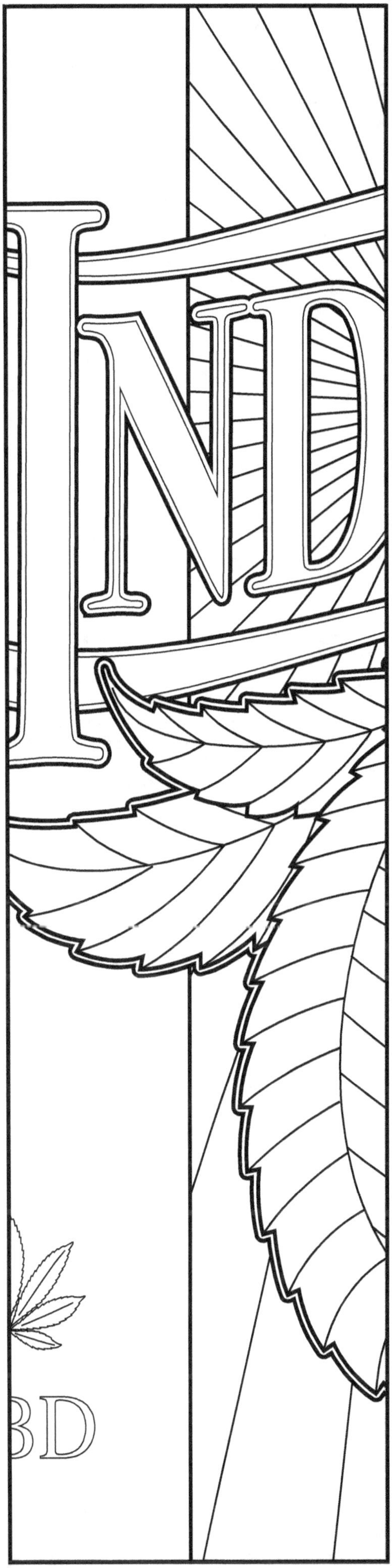

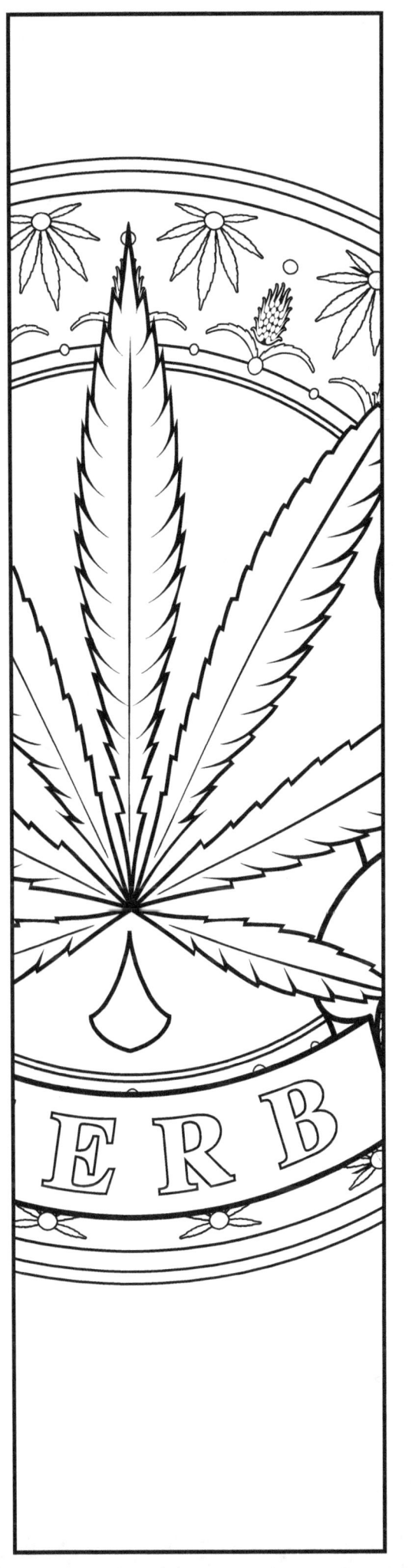
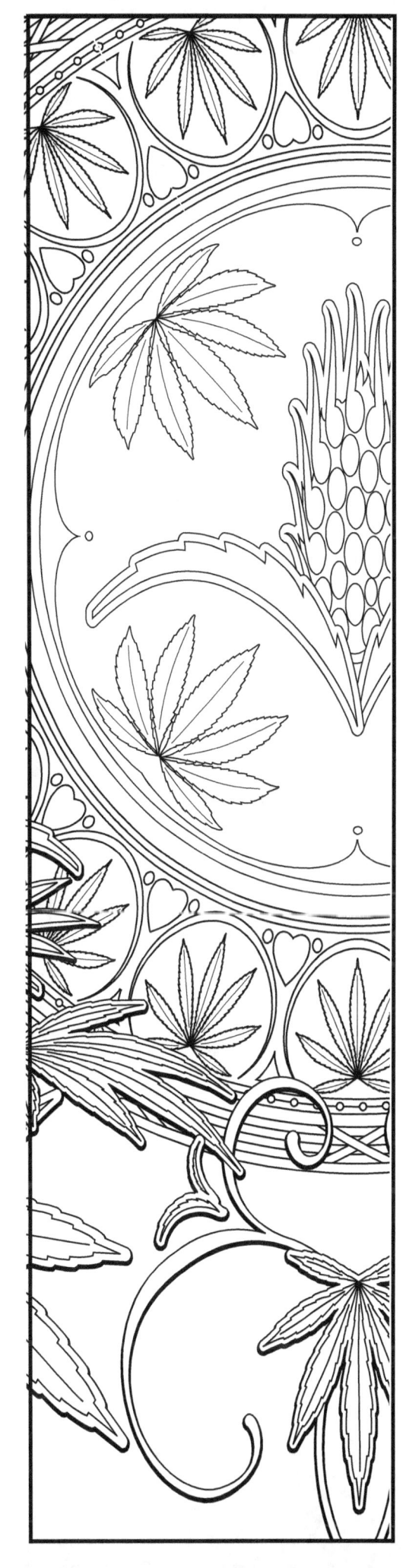

COLOR STUDY STRIPS

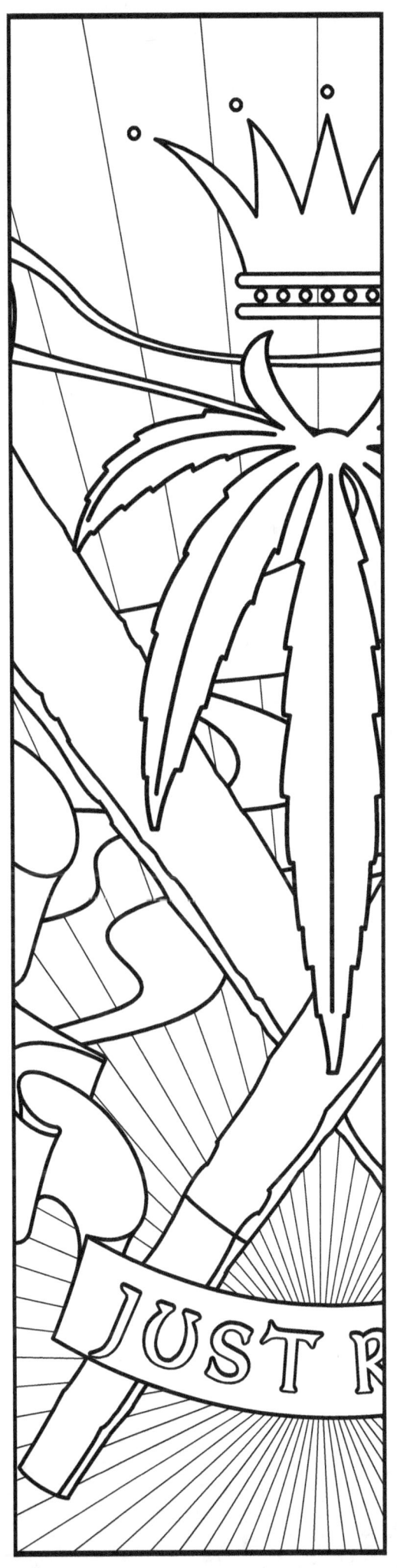

COLOR STUDY STRIPS

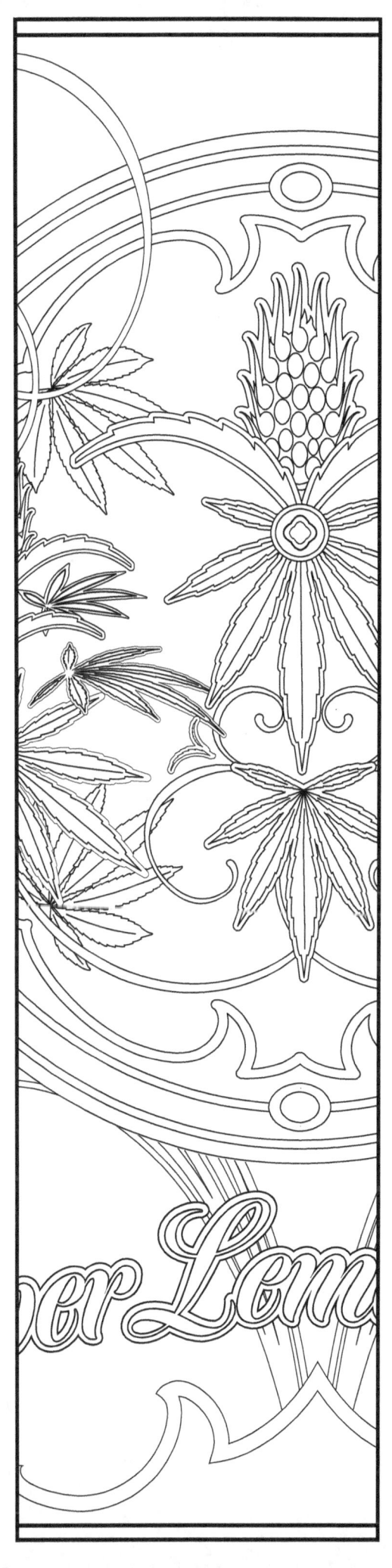

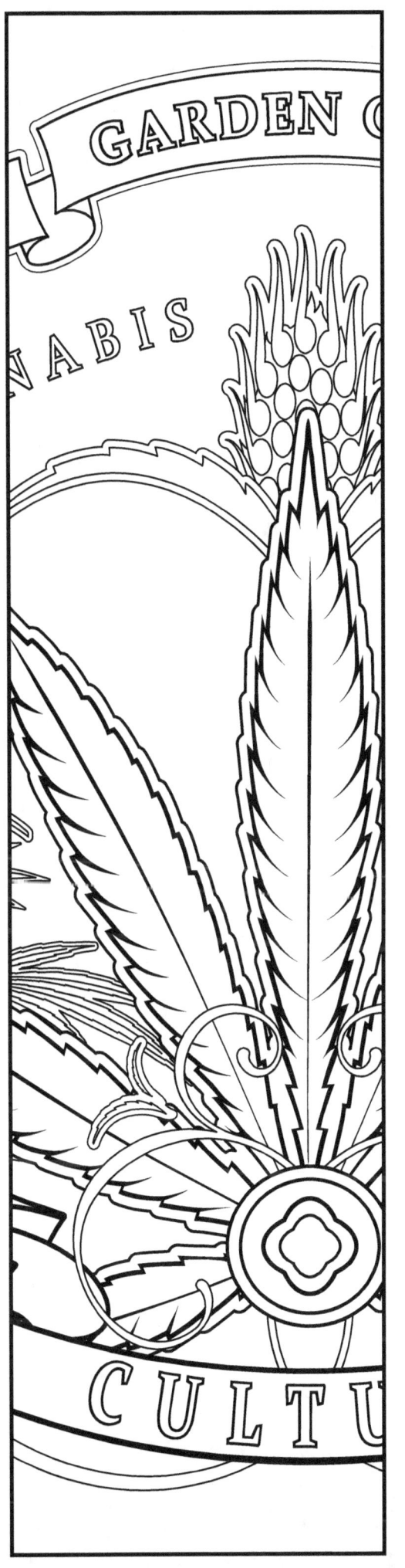

COLOR STUDY STRIPS

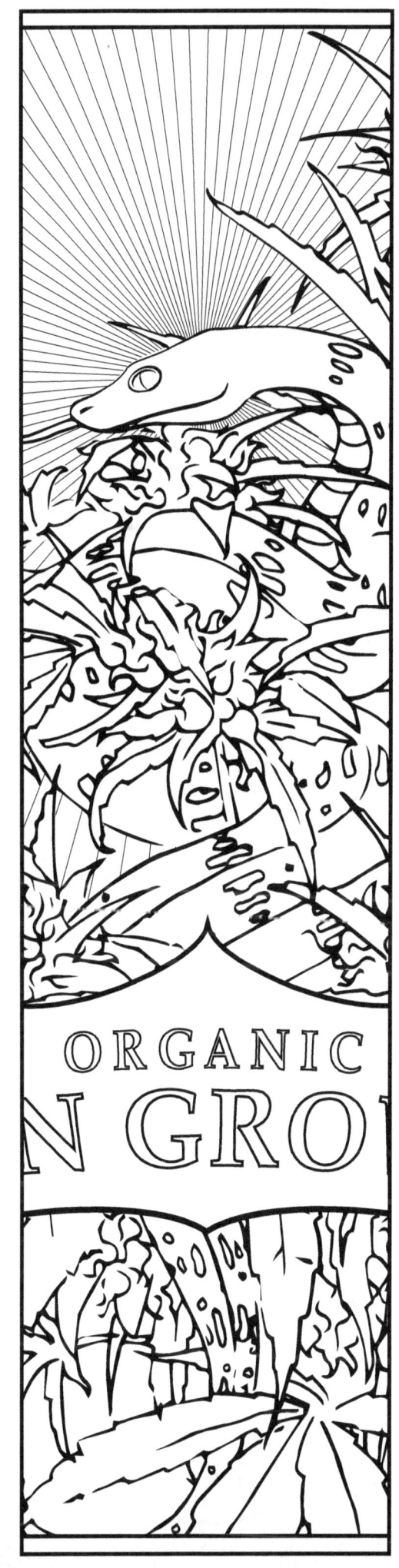

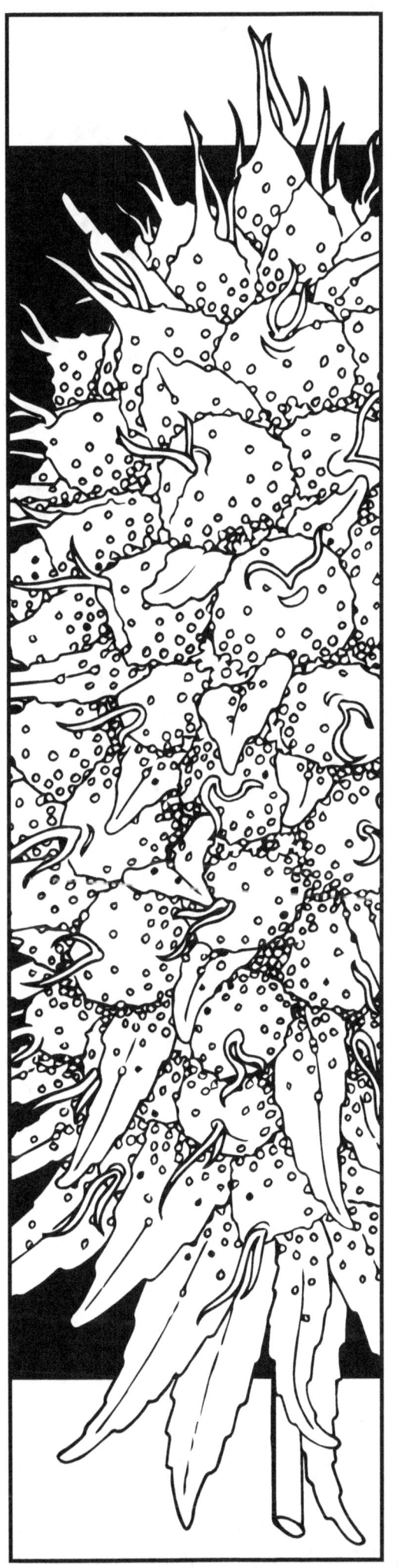

COLOR STUDY STRIPS

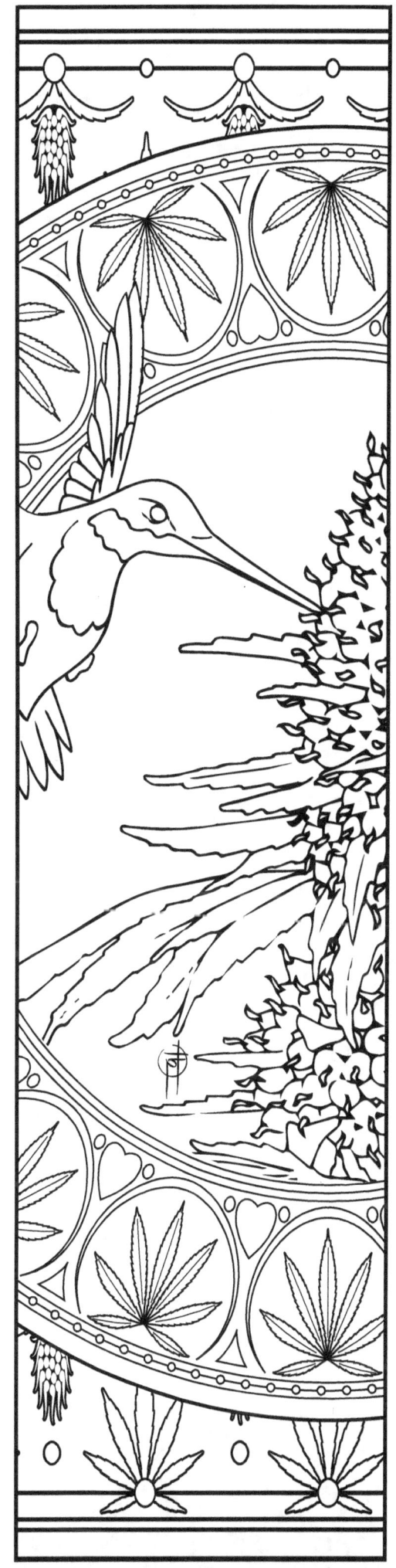

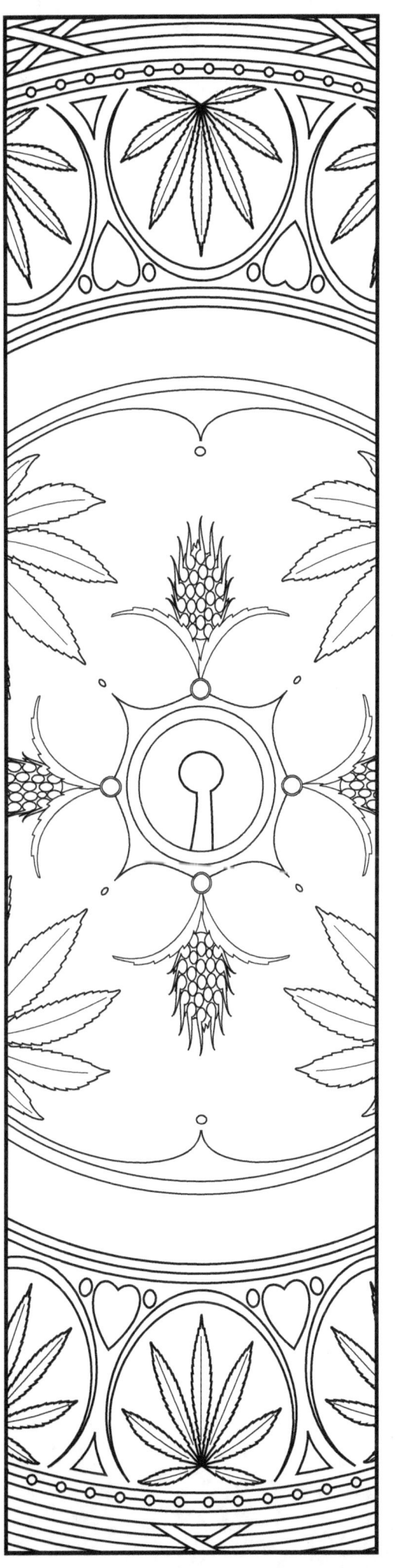

COLOR STUDY STRIPS

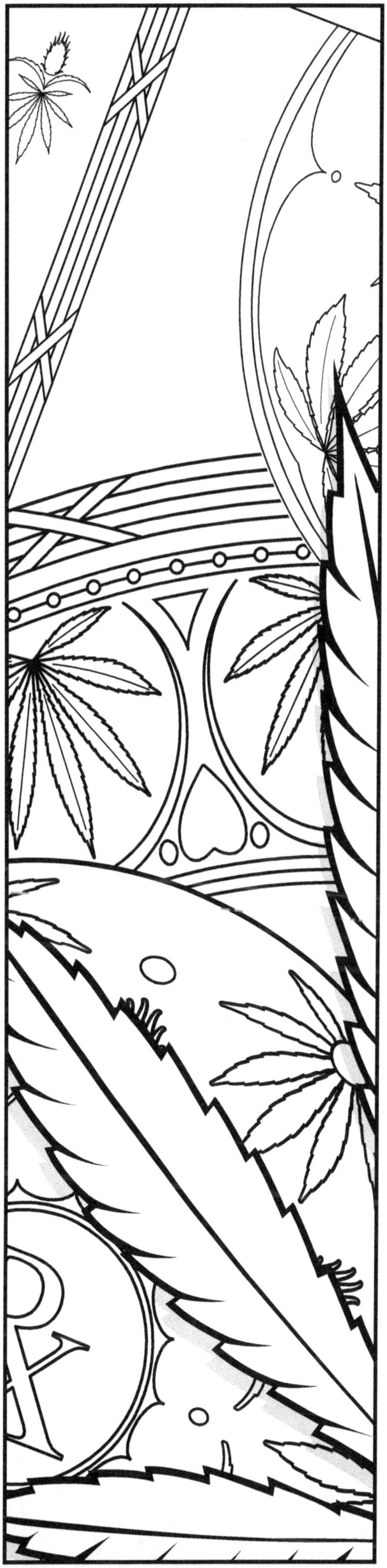

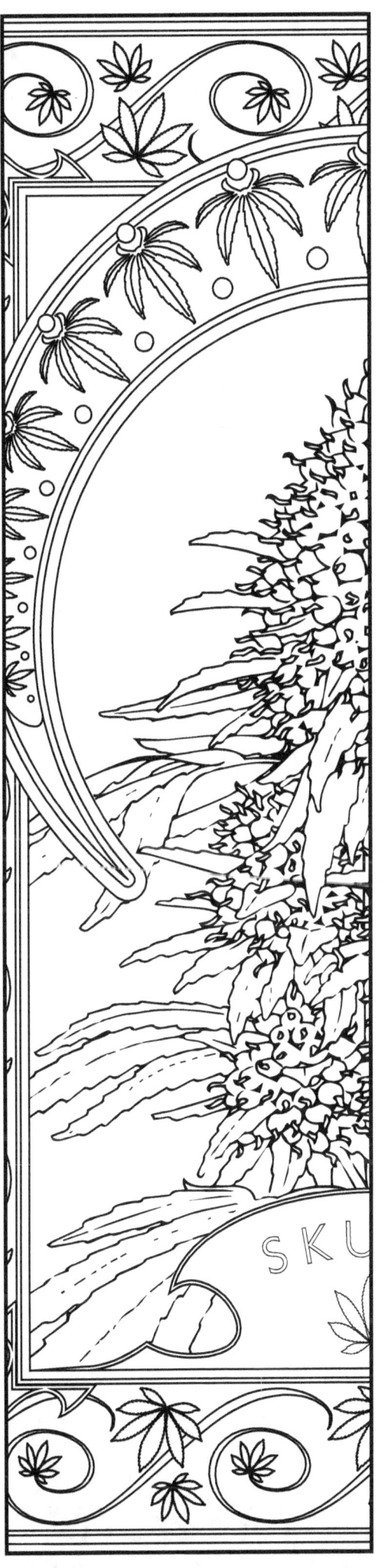

COLOR STUDY STRIPS

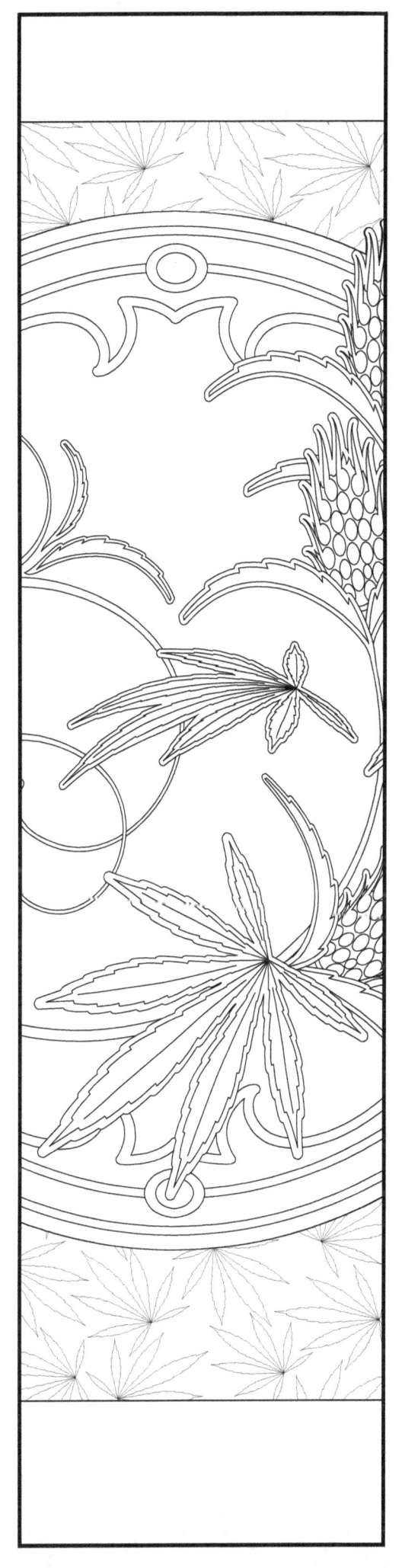

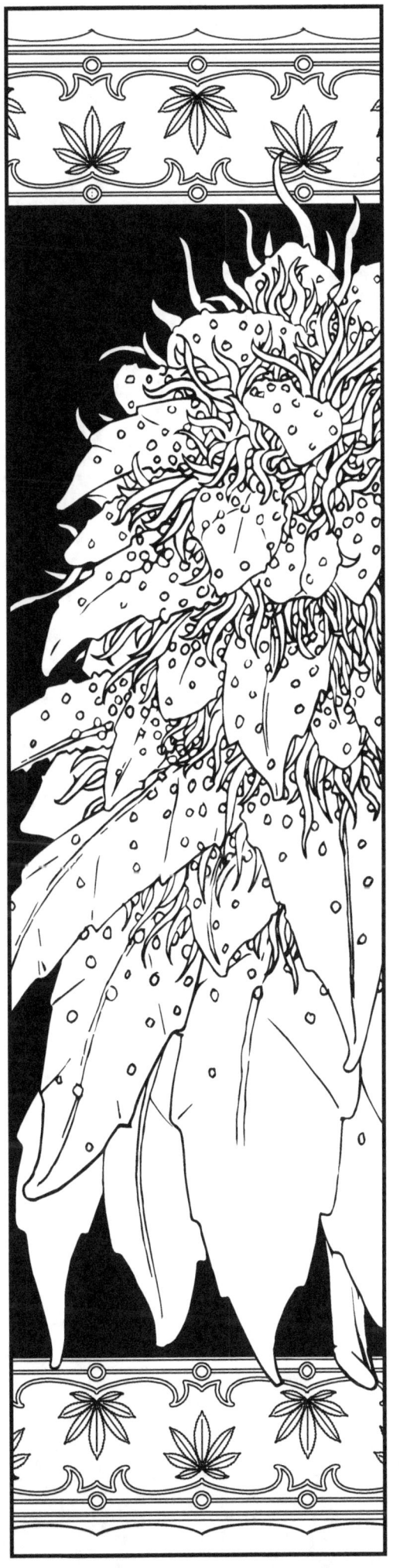

COLOR STUDY STRIPS

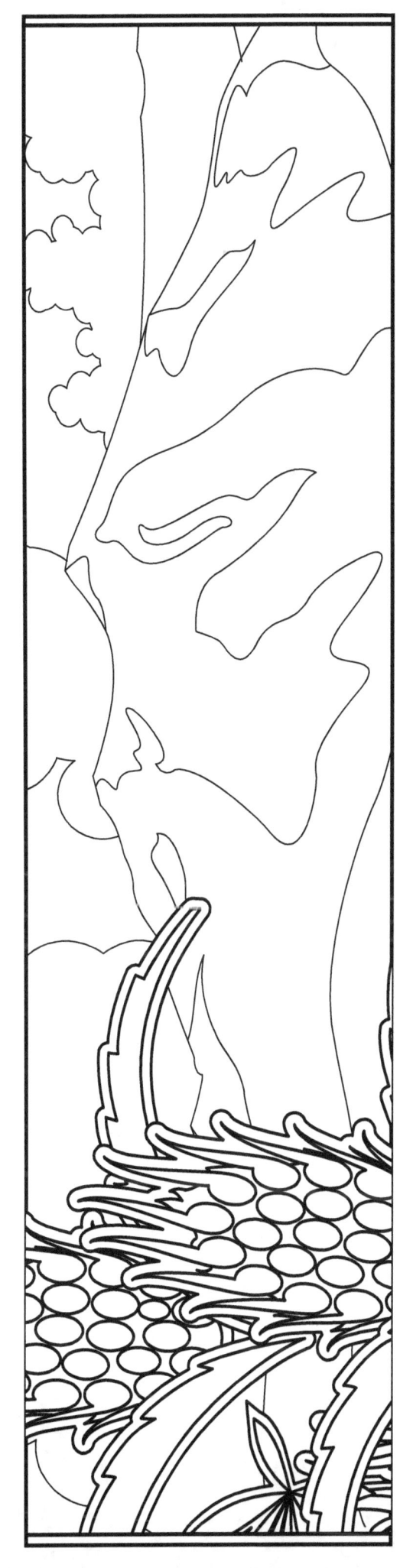

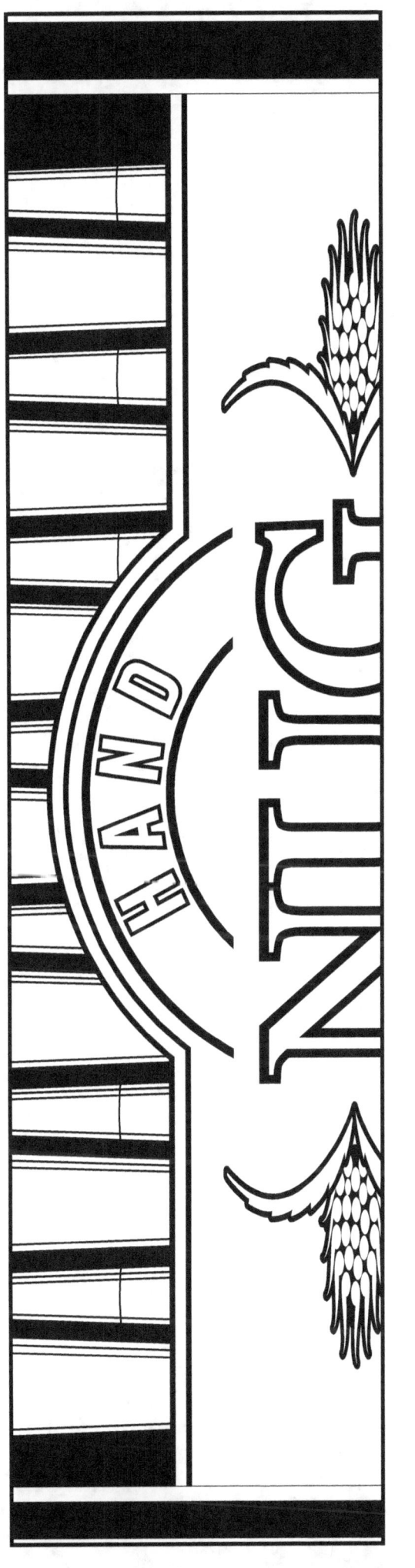
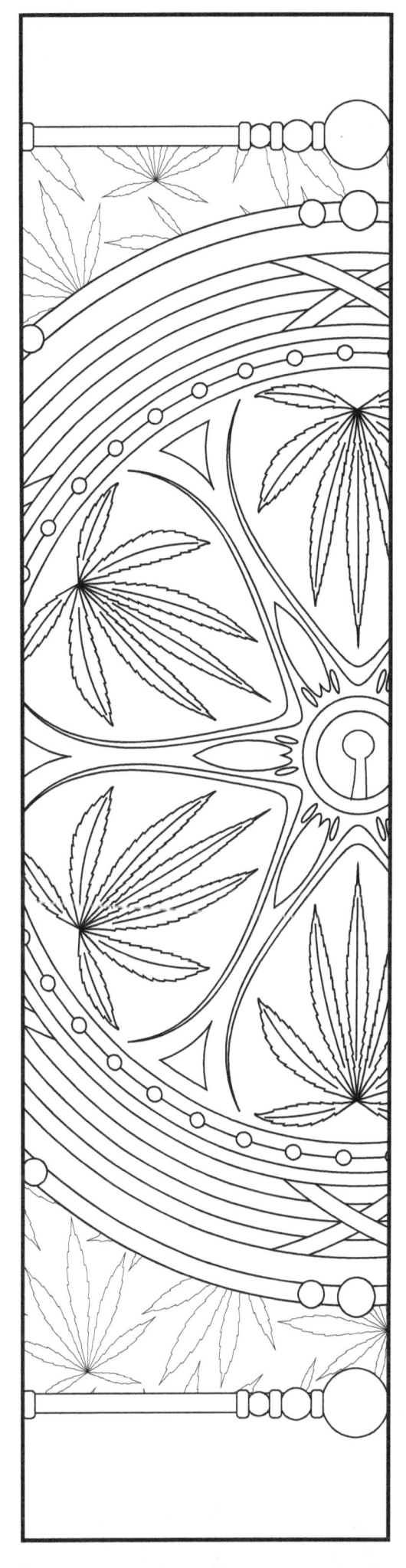

COLOR STUDY STRIPS

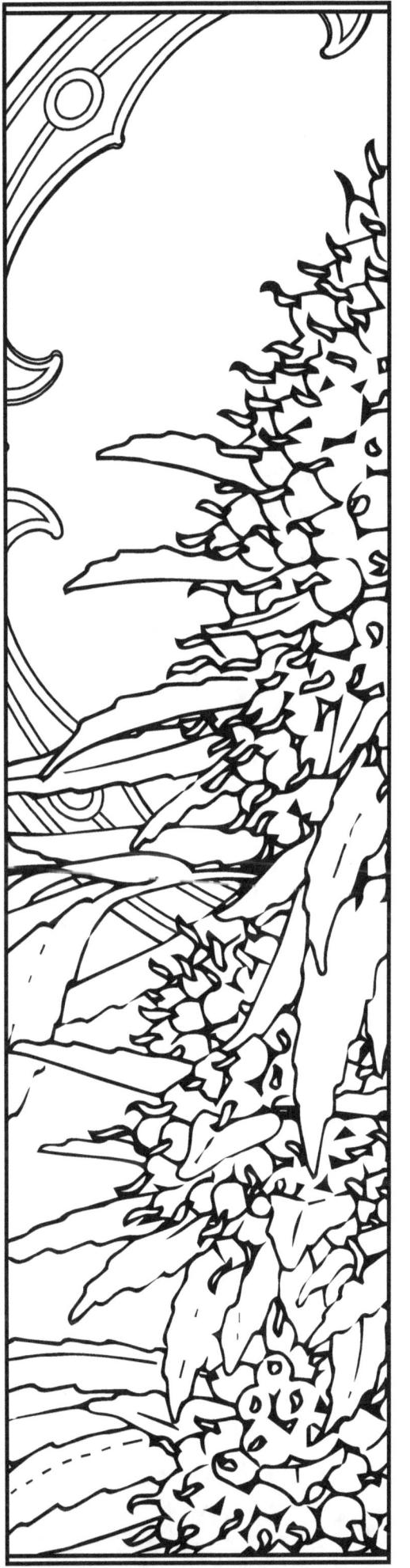
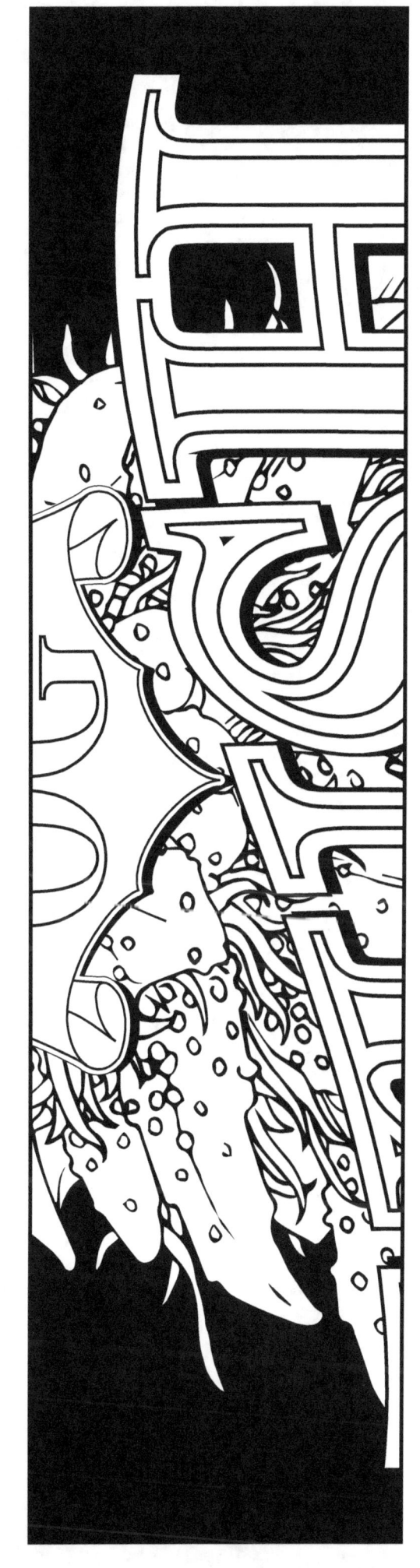

COLOR STUDY STRIPS

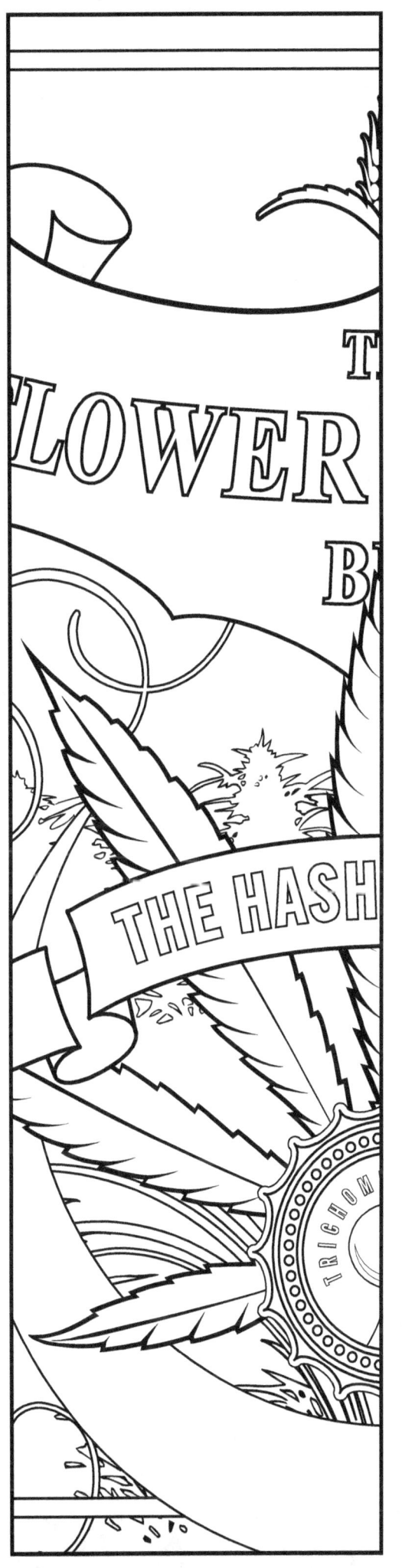

COLOR STUDY STRIPS

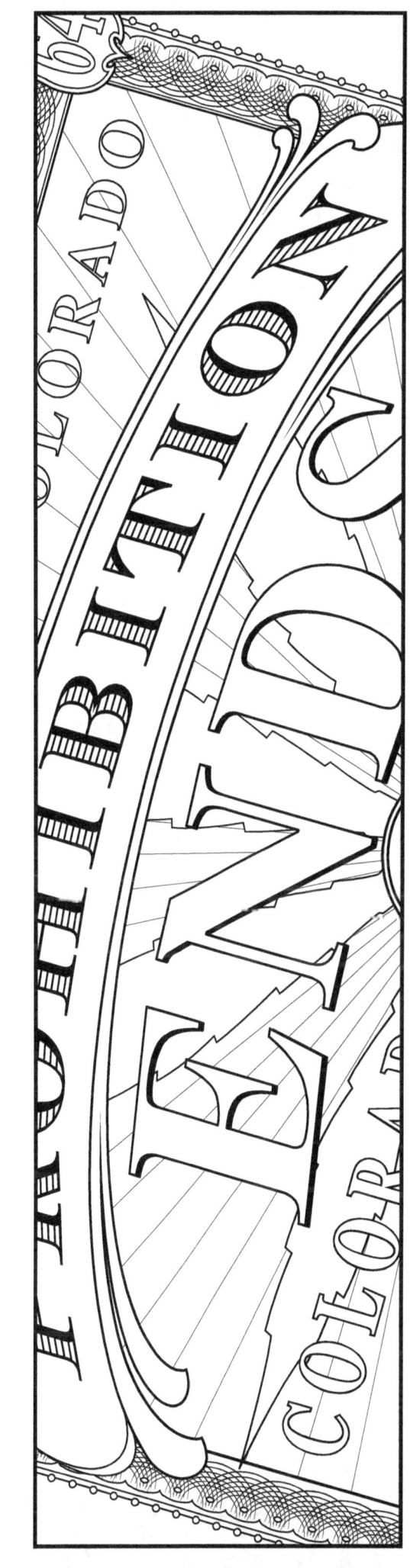

www.ingramcontent.com/pod-product-compliance
Lightning Source LLC
Chambersburg PA
CBHW082214220526
45470CB00010B/3160